Understanding
Welsh
Place Names

"Lovely the woods, waters,

meadows, combes, vales,

All the air things wear that

build this world of Wales."

Gerald Manley Hopkins, In the Valley of the Elwy, 1877

Understanding Welsh Place Names

What they mean and how to say them

Gwili Gog

Northern Eye

Northern Eye Books

www.northerneyebooks.co.uk

First published in 2010 by **Northern Eye Books**,
Castleview, High Street, Cheshire CH3 9PX.

For sales enquiries, please call: 01928 723 744

Copyright © Northern Eye Books 2010.
Northern Eye Books Limited Reg. No. 05460709

www.northerneyebooks.co.uk

ISBN 978-0-9553557-4-5

British Library Cataloguing-in-publication data.
A catalogue is available for this book from the British Library.

Map based on satellite images and out of copyright Ordnance Survey mapping.

Thanks, diolch

This book could not have been written without the kind assistance and support of many people. Warm thanks, in particular, go to Gwen Evans and Dr Harri Roberts, for their indispensable suggestions, insights, and subtle understanding of the Welsh language.

Acknowledgements

The author and publishers are the first to acknowledge that they are 'dwarfs standing on the shoulders of giants'. This popular compilation could not have been produced without the lifelong dedicated researches of numerous eminent Welsh scholars including, among others: Sir Ifor Williams, Professor Melville Richards, Professor Hywel Wyn Owen, Professor Bedwyr Lewis Jones, Professor Gwynedd O Pierce, Richard Morgan, D Geraint Lewis. Thanks are due, too, to the Welsh Language Board for their helpful advice on the preferred place name spelllings. In contrast, any solecisms, errors or omissions are entirely our own.

Thanks, too, to professional blacksmith Matthew Hallett, for kindly agreeing to be photographed at work.

Graphic Design and Maps

Carl Rogers/Northern Eye Books

Photographs

Tony Bowerman, Carl Rogers, Simon Booth, Stefan Lange, Gary Wilson, Shutterstock.

Contents

Themes

Wales
A Land Apart

Foel Goch and Llyn Ogwen, Gwynedd

W ELSH PLACE NAMES are as much a part of the distinct 'otherness' of Wales as its mountains, sheep or gentle rain. They are all around us: in guidebooks, road atlases, maps and road signs. But what exactly do they mean? At first sight, they can seem strangely foreign, confusing or simply unpronounceable. And yet, once carefully unravelled, they can tell us all sorts of fascinating things about a place—its landscape, character and history.

Happily for us, Welsh has changed so little over the last thousand or so years that anyone with even a basic understanding of modern Welsh can begin to translate the majority of Welsh place names. This is in contrast to English, whose place names are often a confusing mish-mash of words from the languages of Roman, Irish, Viking, Saxon and Norman settlers and invaders, Indecipherable today to everyone except linguistic experts.

Apart from some areas along the Welsh/English borders and on the south coast, almost all mountains, hills, valleys, rivers, streams, villages, farms, houses and churches of Wales feature unadulterated native names based on the ancient Celtic Welsh language.

Welsh place names are mostly descriptive. Some describe local features or suggest the essential character of a place. Some refer to a person or saint, or give clues to what a place was like in the past. Others reflect our ancestors' working lives, their beliefs and superstitions, or even deeply held feelings about a place. Together, they help illuminate, and make sense of, this green and pleasant land—bringing the Welsh countryside to life.

Place names can be made up of either one or more elements. Single element place names, for example, include: Bryn (or 'hill'), in Neath Port Talbot; Cwm (or 'valley'), in Denbighshire; and Dinas ('fort' or 'citadel') in Gwynedd. Compound place names can include two, three or more elements, as, for example, in Bryndu (*'hill'* + *'black'*) in Anglesey, or Cwmyreglwys (*'valley'* + *'of the'* + *'church'*) in Pembrokeshire. Translate the individual place name elements, put them back together again and, in most cases, the overall meaning becomes clear.

Of course, there are exceptions. Most place names weren't written down for centuries; dialects vary across Wales, and even locally; pronunciations change over time; words get altered or shortened by mistake, for everyday convenience, or through constant use. And when Welsh place names were eventually recorded by scholars, publishers and map makers—many of whom were English—there were inevitably mishearings, misunderstandings and misspellings. So things are not always what they seem. All the meanings of the place names listed here are taken from reliable academic sources based on the earliest documentary evidence.

But if the real meaning of a few place names remains obscure, a puzzle for future scholars, most are open to translation. For the native Welsh person and English visitor alike, they form a sort of landscape poetry—vivid, romantic and evocative of a wilder past.

"Our country is something alive, not a dead grave under our feet. Every hill has its story, every district its romance ..."

Owen M Edwards, *Adfyfyrion,* 1907

An Ancient Language

WELSH HAS HARDLY CHANGED *in a thousand years. Modern Welsh is surprisingly similar to the language spoken in Wales in pre-Norman times. It's also true that Welsh literary tradition stretches back to the 7th century AD—far longer than any other surviving European language. Yet the origins of Welsh are older still. The language arrived in Britain with the Iron Age Celts in the 4th century BC. Driven westward into the hills by successive waves of Romans, Vikings, Anglo-Saxons, and Normans, their Celtic tongue remained the main language spoken in Wales until the 19th century, when growing trade encouraged the spread of English. Today, the Welsh language is widely spoken and taught in schools, appears on road signs and place names across Wales, is used on television and radio, in newspapers, books, magazines and the internet, and appears on all official documents.*

Snowdon group from Capel Curig, Gwynedd

Pronouncing
Welsh Place Names

A LTHOUGH IT MAY look 'difficult' to the outsider, Welsh is actually a logical language. Unlike English—with all its notorious idiosyncrasies—Welsh spelling and pronunciation are almost entirely regular and phonetic. Learn a few basic rules and you'll find Welsh pronunciation surprisingly simple. One of the main reasons is that all the letters in Welsh words are pronounced; none are ever silent. So what you see is what you say.

It's worth remembering, too, that the emphasis in spoken Welsh is usually on the last but one syllable. So, for example, Beddgelert is pronounced 'beth-**gell**-airt' and Bangor, '**bang**-gor'.

There are 28 letters in the Welsh alphabet: A, B, C, Ch, D, Dd, E, F, FF, G, Ng, H, I, L, Ll, M, N, O. P, Ph, R, Rh, S, T, Th, U, W, Y. Most are the same as in English, but with some notable exceptions and additions.

Firstly, there are no J, K, Q, V, X or Z in traditional Welsh—despite occasional modern 'borrowings' from other languages, as seen in words like jam, Jones (!) or zw ('zoo'). And, secondly, what appear to be 'double consonants'—Ch, Dd, Ff, Ll, Ng, Rh and Th—are actually individual letters, each with their own pronunciation.

"Welsh is of this soil,
this island, the senior
language of the men of
Britain; and Welsh is
beautiful."

JRR Tolkien, *The O'Donell Lecture*, 1955

So let's look at the consonants. B, D, H, L, M, N, P, and T are usually pronounced in the same way as they are in English. H is never silent. But some of the others differ hugely:

C is always a hard 'k' sound, as in 'cat' or 'king'

Ch is always soft and aspirated as in 'Bach' or the Scottish''loch'

Dd always sounds like 'th' as in 'the' or 'thee'

F always sounds like a 'V', as in 'vile'

Ff is always hard as in 'off'

G is always hard as in 'get' or 'give'

Ng sounds like the 'ng' in 'finger' or in 'angst'

Ll is uniquely Welsh, an aspirated 'l', roughly similar to 'thl…'

Rh is trillod, as if the 'h' comes before the 'r'

Th sounds like 'th' as in 'think'

Welsh has seven vowels, as opposed to the usual five in English.

A is usually hard as in 'van'

E is always hard as in 'jet'

I is either hard as in 'pin', or soft as in 'machine'

O is either hard as in 'hot', or soft as in 'hotel'

U sounds like either 'i' or 'ee', and is either hard as in 'it' or soft as in 'feet'

W sounds like 'oo' as in 'zoo'

Y sounds like 'ee' as in 'happy' or 'ur' or 'myrrh'

And finally, under certain conditions, the initial consonant of a word can change so that, for example, coch ('red') becomes goch, moel ('bare hill') becomes foel, and pont ('bridge') becomes bont.

Can yw ryd ddys? Gwd lwc and haf ffwn!

Keywords: Common Welsh Place Name Elements

Aber	river mouth, estuary; where two waters meet	*Abb-er*
Afon	river	*Avv-on*
Allt	slope (N Wales); wooded slope (S Wales)	*Ath-lt*
Aran	high place	*Ar-ran*
Bach	small, little, lesser; corner, river bend	*Back*
Bae	bay	*Bye*
Banc	bank	*Bank*
Bedd	grave, tomb	*Be-th*
Bedwen	birch tree	*Bed-wen*
Betws	prayer house, oratory, chapel of ease	*Bet-oos*
Blaen	head of a valley; source of a river	*Bline*
Bod	home, dwelling; church	*Bod*
Bron	breast; rounded hillside	*B-ron*
Bryn	hill	*Bri-n*
Bwlch	mountain pass, gap	*Bool-k*
Cae	field, enclosure	*Kye*
Caer	fort, fortified settlement	*Kye-r*
Capel	non-conformist meeting house, chapel	*Kap-el*
Canol	centre, middle	*Kan-ol*
Castell	castle; fortified town; prominent rock	*Kast-e-th*
Carrog	swift stream, torrent	*Kar-rog*
Carreg	stone, rock	*Kar-reg*
Carn, carnedd	heap of stones; cairn, tumulus	*Kar-neth*
Cartref	home	*Kar-trev*
Cefn	ridge	*Kev-enn*
Cil	corner, recess, nook, shelter	*Kill*
Clogwyn	steep cliff	*Klog-win*
Clun	meadow, moor; brushwood	*Klun*
Coch	red	*Koch*
Coed	wood, forest, trees	*Koyd*
Copa	top, crest, summit	*Kop-a*
Cors	fen, bog, marsh	*Kors*
Craig	rock, boulder, crag	*Krye-g*
Croes	cross; crossroads	*Kroys*

Crug	heap, pile of stones	*Krig*
Cwm	coombe, valley	*Koom*
Cymer	confluence	*Kummer*
Dan/tan	below, under	*Dan*
Derwen	oak tree	*Dare-wen*
Du/ddu	black; shaded	*Dee/Thee*
Din/dinas	citadel; hillfort; fortified hill	*Din/Din-as*
Dŵr/dwfr	water	*Doo-er*
Dyffryn	valley; bottom	*Duff-rin*
Eglwys	church	*Egg-lewis*
Esgair	ridge, mountain spur	*Es-gair*
Felin	mill	*Ve-lin*
Fferm	farm	*Ferm*
Ffordd	road, way	*For-th*
Ffridd	rough mountain pasture, sheep walk	*Freeth*
Ffynnon	well; spring; fountain; source	*Fun-non*
Foel	bare hill	*Voyel*

Ancestral Spirits?

PREHISTORIC SITES ACROSS WALES *are often associated with myth and superstition. A Neolithic burial chamber in Anglesey is rightly named Bryn yr Hen Bobl, (or 'hill of the old people'). But elsewhere, prehistoric monuments were thought to belong to giants, goblins and witches. Beddau'r Cowri, in Powys, means 'the giants' graves'; Bryn-yr-Ellyllon, in Flintshire, means 'hill of the goblins'; and Arffedogaid y Wrach, in Denbighshire, translates as 'the witch's apronful'. Other prehistoric burial chambers, such as Coetan Arthur, in Pembrokeshire, were named after legendary kings and heroes.*

Gardd	garden, enclosure	*Gar-th*
Gelli	grove	*Ge-thlee*
Glan	river bank, shore, edge	*Glan*
Glyn	narrow valley, glen, dingle	*Glun*
Goleudy	lighthouse	*Gol-eye-dee*
Gorsaf	station	*Gorsav*
Gwastad	flat	*Gwas-tad*
Gwaun/waun	moor, low marshy ground	*Gwine*
Gwlad	country	*Goo-lad*
Gwyn	white; blessed, holy	*Gwin*
Haf	summer	*Hav*
Hafod/hafoty	upland farm for summer grazing	*Hav-vod*
Hen	old, ancient; former	*Hen*
Hendre	old or former house; winter settlement	*Hen-dre*
Heol	road, way	*Hoyl*
Hir	long	*Her*
Isaf	lower; lowest	*Ees-av*
Llan	enclosure, early church; parish church	*Thl-an*
Lle	place	*Thl-e*
Llech	flat stone, flagstone, slate	*Thl-eck*
Llechwedd	hillside	*Thl-eck-weth*
Llwybr	path	*Thloo-u-ber*
Llwyd	grey, pale; russet, brown	*Thl-oo-ud*
Llwyn	grove, bush	*Thl-oo-un*
Llyn	lake; large pool	*Thl-in*
Llys	manor house, hall; court	*Thl-us*
Maen	stone; standing stone	*Mine*
Maes	plain, open unwooded country; field	*Myse*
Maerdy	dairy farm, home farm	*My-er-dee*
Marchnad	market	*Mark-nad*
Mawr	big, large, great	*Maw-er*
Melin	mill	*Mel-in*
Merthyr	shrine; saint's burial place	*Merth-er*
Moel	barren; bald; bare or rounded hill	*Moyle*
Môr	sea	*Moor*
Morfa	salt marsh, coastal marsh	*More-va*
Mwyn	mine, mineral ore	*Moo-un*
Mynachlog	monastery	*Mun-ack-log*
Mynydd	mountain, hill; unenclosed mountain land	*Munn-uth*
Nant	stream, brook; stream valley	*Nant*
Neuadd	hall	*Nee-ath*

Newydd	new	*Neh-with*
Ogof	cave, cavern	*Ogov*
Pant	hollow, valley	*Pant*
Parc	enclosed land, field; parkland	*Park*
Parrog	flat land by the sea	*Pa-rog*
Pen	head, main, chief; top of a valley	*Pen*
Pentref	hamlet, village	*Pen-trev*
Pistyll	spring, waterfall; well	*Pist-ith*
Plas	hall, mansion	*Plass*
Pont/bont	bridge, arch	*Pont*
Porth	harbour, port, gateway	*Por-th*
Pwll	pool, pit	*Poo-thl*
Rhiw	steep hillside, ascent	*Thl-eck*
Rhôs	moor, upland, heath	*Roe-s*
Rhyd	ford; river crossing place	*Rhee-d*
Sant	saint	*Sant*
Sarn	paved way, causeway; stepping stones	*Sarn*
Tal	end, front	*Tal*

The Body of the Land

AS WITH MANY OTHER ANCIENT LANGUAGES, *Welsh often likens the shape of the land to parts of the human body. Place name elements in particular reflect this poetic way of thinking. Common examples include pen (meaning 'head' or 'top'), as in Penmaenmawr, and cefn (meaning 'back' or 'ridge'), as in Cefn-y-Bedd. Other bodily words used to describe the landscape include moel (meaning 'bald' or 'naked') for a bare hill, braich (or 'arm') and esgair (or 'leg') for a mountain ridge, gwar ('nape') for a ridge or neck of land, trwyn ('nose') and tal (or 'forehead') for a headland, cesail ('armpit') for a hollow, and bron (or 'breast') for a rounded hillside. Watch out too for the irreverent use of cest or gest ('fat belly') to describe a protruding hillside or headland, as in Borth-y-Gest, near Porthmadog.*

Tomen	mound, heap	*Tom-en*
Traeth	beach, shore	*Try-th*
Tref	settlement, farm; village, town	*Tre-v*
Trum	ridge	*Trum*
Tŵr	tower, keep	*Too-er*
Tŷ	house, houses	*Tee*
Tyddyn	croft, smallholding	*Tuth-un*
Uchaf	highest, upper	*Ick-av*
Uwch	beyond, higher	*Ooch*
Y/Yr	the/of the	*Err/Urr*
Ysbyty	hospital	*Us-but-ty*
Ystrad	valley, vale, river-meadow	*Us-trad*
Ynys	island, isle; holm	*Unnis*

"Let nobody imagine that because there is so much English in Wales, it is not a foreign language."

RS Thomas, in *Planet*, 1978

"If we are to understand
the history of Wales, and
to know the Welshman's
soul, we have to start
with the mountains."

Owen M Edwards, in *Cymru*, 1891

Tryfan, Ogwen valley, Gwynedd

Describing the Land

In the Mountains

Adwy	breach, gap	*Add-weet*
Allt	hill, hillside, slope, wooded slope	*Al-th-t*
Anial	wild, deserted, desolate	*An-ial*
Aran	high place	*A-ran*
Ardd	hill, height, high land	*Ar-th*
Ban	cow's horn; horn-like peak, crest, beacon	*Ban*
Boncyn	hillock	*Bonk-un*
Braich	ridge, arm	*Bray-ch*
Bre	hill	*Bray*
Bron	breast; rounded hillside	*Bron*
Bryn	hill, mountain	*Brin*
Bwlch	mountain pass, gap	*Bool-k*
Carn	cairn, mound; barrow, tumulus	*Karn*
Carnedd	cairn, heap of stones; burial mound, tumulus	*Karn-eth*
Carreg	stone, rock	*Karreg*
Cefn	back, ridge	*Kev-in*
Cerwyn	vat, tub; pothole	*Ker-win*
Cesail	hollow	*Kes-ile*
Clog	crag, cliff, precipice, steep slope	*Klog*
Clegyr	rock, cliff	*Kleg-er*
Clip	crag, precipice, steep slope	*Klip*
Copa	crest, summit	*Koppa*
Crib	ridge, crest, arete	*Krib*
Crug	hillock; cairn, heap of stones	*Krig*
Cwm	coombe, valley	*Koom*
Cyfrwy	saddle, ridge between two summits	*Kuv-roo-ee*
Dysgl	dish	*Dis-gul*
Dibyn	precipice, steep slope	*Dub-in*
Diffwys	precipice, cliff, desolate place	*Duf-wis*
Drws	pass, gap, narrow doorway	*Droos*
Drum	mountain crest, ridge	*Drim*
Eifl	forked peak	*Eye-val*
Eira	snow	*Eye-ra*
Eryri	eagle's realm; highland	*E-ru-ree*
Esgair	long ridge, mountain spur	*Es-gair*
Gloddfa	quarry	*Gloth-fa*
Gogerdd	steps, ledges, terraces	*Gog-erth*

Grisiau	steps, ledges, terraces	*Griss-eye*
Grug	heath, heather	*Grig*
Gwaun	wet moorland; low marshy ground; meadow	*Gwine*
Gwar	nape of the neck; ridge	*Gwar*
Hafn	gap, ravine, gorge	*Hav-n*
Llechog	rocky	*Thleck-hog*
Llethr	slope	*Thleth-er*
Mawnog	peat bog	*Maw-nog*
Moel	bald or barren; bare or rounded hill	*Moy-l*
Mynydd	mountain; moorland; unenclosed land	*Munn-uth*
Rhinog	threshold	*Rhinn-og*
Rhiw	hill, slope	*Roo*
Rhos	moor; promontory, headland	*Roe-s*
Rhyn	promontory	*Run*
Tarren	escarpment, scarp slope	*Tarr-en*
Trum	ridge	*Trim*
Ystlys	side, flank	*Ust-liss*

Hills and Mountains

WALES IS A LAND OF HILLS *and mountains. So it's to be expected that Welsh has so many words describing the subtleties and nuances of slopes and high ground. This richness probably reflects the once intimate relationship between a country people and the landscape they worked. Common Welsh words for hills include* moel, *a 'bare' or 'rounded hill',* mynydd, *'mountain' or 'moorland',* rhos, *also meaning 'moorland', and* rhiw, *for a slope or hill.* Bryn *also means a 'hill' or 'mountain', and* bron *a 'breast' or 'rounded hill'. Similarly,* aran *means a 'high place',* cefn *a 'ridge', and* crib *a 'ridge' or 'crest'. But words like* allt *have subtly different meanings in different parts of Wales: in the north it simply means a 'hillside', whereas in the south* allt *implies a 'wooded slope'.*

In the Valleys

Bargod	boundary, border	*Bar-god*
Bedwen	birch tree	*Bed-wen*
Beidr	lane, track, path	*Bye-der*
Beili	yard	*Bye-lee*
Berllan	orchard	*Ber-thlan*
Berth	bush, hedge	*Berth*
Beudy	cow-house	*Bye-dee*
Bod	home, abode, dwelling	*Bod*
Boncyn	hillock	*Bon-kun*
Borfa	pasture	*Bor-va*
Braenar	fallow land	*Brye-nar*
Bren	timber	*Bren*
Bro	lowland, vale, region	*Bro*
Brwyn	rushes	*Broo-in*
Bugeildy	shepherd's hut	*Big-eyel-dee*
Bwbach	fairy, goblin	*Boo-bach*
Bwll	pit, pool	*Boo-th*

Woods and Trees

Trees once covered far more *of Wales than they do today. Woods and trees occur regularly in Welsh place names. The Welsh for a wood is* coed, *as in* Coed-y-Brenin, *'King's wood'. Individual tree names are common too. Oak (*derwen *or plural,* derw*) place names include* Derwen Fawr, *'great oak', and* Derwen-gam, *or 'crooked oak'. The birch (*bedwen *or plural,* bedw*) regularly crops up too, in names like* Craigfedwen *('birch rock'); while* Bedwlwyn *means 'grove of birches'. The rowan tree (*cerddinen*) occurs in* Ffos y Gerddinen *('ditch of the rowan'); and hawthorn (*draenen*) in* Y Draenen Wen *('the white thorn') and* Ffynnon-ddrain *('hawthorn well'). Look out, too, for other place names incorporating the holly (*celynen*), hazel (*collen*), willow (*helygen*), and yew (*ywen*).*

Bwthyn	cottage	*Buth-in*
Caban	cabin, cottage	*Kab-an*
Cadw	spinney, preserve	*Kad-oo*
Cae	field, enclosure	*K-eye*
Carn	cairn, heap of stones, tumulus	*Karn*
Carreg	stone, rock	*Karr-eg*
Celli/gelli	grove	*Ke-thlee*
Celynen	holly tree	*Kely-nen*
Cerddin	rowan, mountain-ash tree	*Ker-thin*
Clawdd	dyke, bank, ditch, hedge	*Klaw-th*
Clun	meadow, moor	*Klin*
Clwyd	hurdle, gate	*Kloo-id*
Coed	wood, forest, trees	*Koyd*
Coedlan	copse, coppice, woodland glade	*Koyd-lan*
Coety	house in a wood	*Koyd-tee*
Collen	hazel tree	*Ko-thlen*
Colomendy	dovecote	*Kolo-men-dee*
Corlan	sheepfold	*Kor-lan*
Craf	wild garlic	*Krav*
Criafol	rowan, mountain ash tree	*Kree-a-vol*
Cut	shed, pigsty	*Kit*
Dol	meadow, water meadow	*Dol*
Dafad	sheep	*Dav-add*
Dafadfa	sheepfold	*Dav-add-va*
Derwen	oak tree	*Derwen*
Drain	thorn, bramble	*Dryne*
Draenllwyn	thorn or bramble-patch	*Dryne-thloo-in*
Efail	smithy	*Ev-eye-l*
Eiddew	ivy	*Eye-thew*
Eithin	gorse, furze	*Eeth-in*
Ffald	sheepfold, pen	*Fald*
Ffawydden	beech tree	*Faw-u-then*
Ffawyddog	beech grove	*Faw-u-thog*
Fferm	farm	*Ferm*
Glyn	glen, deep valley	*Glun*
Gwair	hay	*Gw-eye-er*
Gwal	den, lair	*Gwarl*
Gwden	willow tree, reeds	*Goo-den*
Gweirglodd	hay field, meadow	*Gwire-gloth*
Gwern	alder tree, damp place of alders	*Gwern*
Gwig	grove	*Gwug*

Gwlad	country	*Goo-lad*
Gwndwn	grassland, meadow	*Gun-doon*
Helygen	willow tree	*Hel-ug-en*
Hendre	winter dwelling, old or permanent home	*Hen-dree*
Hesg	rushes	*Hess-g*
Llaethdy	dairy, milking shed	*Thl-eye-th-dee*
Llannerch	woodland clearing, glade	*Thlan-erk*
Llawr	low ground, valley floor	*Thlawer*
Llidiard	gate	*Thludy-ard*
Lloc	pen, sheep or animal fold	*Thloc*
Lluest	shepherd's hut, shieling	*Thleyest*
Llwyfen	elm tree	*Thloo-u-ven*
Maes	field, open land, plain, territory	*Mise*
Mign	marsh, bog, mire	*Mig-n*
Morfa	marsh, sea marsh, fen	*Mor-va*
Onn	ash tree	*On*
Parc	field	*Park*
Trallwng	wet low-lying land	*Tra-thloong*
Ysgubor	barn	*Us-gib-or*
Ystrad	wide valley	*Us-trad*

By the Water

Afon	river	*Avon*
Bad	ferry, boat	*Bad*
Bala	narrow land between two lakes	*Bal-a*
Berw	foam, rushing water	*Ber-oo*
Blaen	source of a stream	*Bline*
Cafn	ferry boat	*Kav-n*
Carrog	fast-flowing stream, torrent	*Karrog*
Camas	bend, bend in the river	*Kamas*
Ceulan	river bank	*Kee-lan*
Ceunant	gorge, ravine	*Kee-nant*
Cil	nook, corner, recess	*Kill*
Cors	bog, marsh	*Kors*
Cryw	weir, fish trap	*Krew*
Cymer	where two waters meet; confluence	*Kummer*
Dwr	water	*Doo-er*
Dyffryn	flat river valley	*Duff-ryn*
Gabal	ferry boat	*Gabal*
Geirw	waterfall, rushing water	*Gear-oo*

Glan	bank, river bank	*Glan*
Gofer	overflow from a well, rill	*Gov-er*
Hafan	haven, harbour	*Havan*
Llech	flat stone, slab, slate	*Thleck*
Llethr	slope, steep descent	*Thleth-er*
Llwch	lake; marsh or mire	*Thlook*
Llwng	wetland	*Thloong*
Llyr	sea, water	*Thler*
Mign	marsh, bog	*Mig-n*
Nant	stream, small river, river valley	*Nant*
Pistyll	spout, spring, well	*Piss-tith*
Rhaeadr	waterfall, cascade	*Rye-adder*
Rhyd	ford, river crossing	*Reed*
Sgwd	(S Wales) waterfall	*Sgood*
Ystum	bend, meander	*Ust-um*

Bogs and Marshes

AS A COUNTRY OF HILLS AND MOUNTAINS, *Wales is renowned for its rain, rivers and streams. Before the days of modern agricultural drainage, running water often spread across the waterlogged lowlands as mire, marsh and bog. A quick look at Welsh place names on the map shows how widespread these wetlands once were. Common Welsh wetland words include* cors *(or 'bog')*, mawnog *('peat bog')*, gwaun *('wet moorland')*, *and* gwern *(or 'marsh')*. Llwng *or* llong *means wetland, too. Less common is the Welsh word* mign. *The Migneint is a vast tract of high boggy land near Ysbyty Ifan in North Wales whose name derives from* mign *and* neint—*an older form of* nant, *meaning a stream valley.*

Common frogs, Glyn Ceiriog, Wrexham

On the Coast

Aber	river mouth, estuary	*Ab-er*
Bae	bay	*Bye*
Cawl	sea kale	*Kowl*
Cei	quay	*Key*
Cilfach	cove, creek	*Kill-vak*
Clegyr	rock, cliff	*Klegg-er*
Culfor	strait	*Kill-vor*
Goleudy	lighthouse	*Gol-eye-dee*
Glan	shore	*Glan*
Gwymon	seaweed	*Goo-u-mon*
Harbwr	harbour	*Har-boor*
Heli	salt water, brine	*Helly*
Môr	sea, ocean	*More*
Morfa	sea marsh, salt marsh	*Moor-va*
Moryd	estuary, channel	*Moor-ud*
Ogof	cave	*Og-ov*
Parrog	flat land by the sea	*Pa-rog*
Penrhyn	headland	*Pen-ryn*
Pigyn	point	*Pig-in*
Porth	harbour	*Porth*
Pwll	pool, pit	*Poo-thl*
Tafol	dock	*Tav-ol*
Ton/don	wave	*Tonn*
Traeth	beach	*Try-th*
Trwyn	nose; point, cape	*Troo-in*
Tywyn	sandy shore; sand dunes	*Too-in*
Ynys	island	*Unnus*

Church and Chapel

Abad	abbot	*Ab-add*
Bangor	enclosure with wattle fence	*Bang-or*
Basaleg	church, basilica	*Bas-a-leg*
Bendigaid	blessed	*Ben-dig-aid*
Betws	prayer house, oratory, chapel of ease	*Bet-oos*
Capel	chapel of ease; nonconformist chapel	*Kap-el*
Cloch	bell	*Klock*
Clochydd	parish clerk, sexton	*Klock-uth*
Croes	cross, crossroads	*Kroys*
Cythraul	devil	*Kuth-raul*

Diserth	hermitage; wilderness	*Dis-erth*
Drindod	trinity	*Drin-dod*
Eglwys	church	*Eg-loo-is*
Esgob	bishop	*Es-gob*
Gwynfa	paradise	*Gwin-va*
Llan	clearing, enclosure; early church, church	*Thlan*
Manachlog	monastery, abbey	*Man-ack-log*
Merthyr	martyr, burial place, church	*Merther*
Meudwy	hermit	*Meye-doo-ey*
Mynach	monk	*Min-ack*
Mynachdy	monastic grange or farm	*Min-ack-dee*
Mynachlog	monastery	*Min-ack-log*
Mynwent	churchyard, burial ground, cemetery	*Min-went*
Nawdd	sanctuary	*Now-th*
Noddfa	sanctuary	*Noth-va*
Offeiriad	priest	*Off-hay-eer-iad*
Plwyf	parish	*Ploo-uv*
Sant	saint	*Sant*

Ancient Animals

THE CELTS HAD A DEEP RESPECT *for animals—both wild and domestic. Many of these creatures were worshipped in the old religions. Sacred animals included the horse, wolf, bear, boar, and eagle. By adopting the name of an animal, warriors believed they also took on some of their power. Popular names included Arthur, from* arth *(or 'bear'), and Bleddyn, from* blaidd *(or 'wolf'). Special places were often named after animals too. Welsh horse names include Castell March in Gwynedd ('stronghold of the horse') and Moel Meirch in Gwynedd ('bare hill of horses'). Wolves crop up in Coed-y-bleiddiau ('wolves' wood') in Gwynedd and Pwll-y-blaidd ('wolf pit') in Powys. Finally, eagle names include Allt-yr-Eryr ('eagle hillside'), in Powys.*

Birds and Beasts

Aderyn	bird	*Ad-air-in*
Afanc	beaver	*Av-ank*
Aig	shoal of fish	*Eye-g*
Arth	bear	*Are-th*
Barcud	red kite	*Bar-kid*
Banu	piglet	*Ban-ee*
Bela	pine marten	*Bella*
Bery	bird of prey, kite	*Berry*
Blaidd	wolf	*Bly-th*
Bwncath	buzzard	*Boon-kath*
Bran	crow, rook, raven	*Bran*
Bronwen	weasel	*Bron-wen*
Bual	bison	*Bee-al*
Buwch	cow	*Bee-ook*
Bwn	bittern	*Boon*
Carw	wild deer, hart, stag	*Ka-roo*
Caseg	mare	*Kass-eg*
Cath	cat	*Kath*
Ceiliog	cock	*Kee-lee-og*
Ceinach	hare	*Kee-nack*
Ci	dog, hound	*Kee*
Cigfran	raven	*Kig-fran*
Cog	cuckoo	*Kog*
Colomen	dove	*Koll-oh-men*
Colwyn	young animal; puppy	*Koll-win*
Dafad	sheep	*Dav-add*
Danas	deer	*Dan-as*
Dyfrgi	otter	*Duv-er-gee*
Eog	salmon	*Ee-og*
Eos	nightingale	*Ee-oss*
Eryr	eagle	*Err-er*
Ewig	hind (female deer)	*E-wig*
Gafr	goat	*Gav-er*
Gwadd	mole	*Goo-ath*
Gwalch	hawk	*Goo-alck*
Gwenyn	bees	*Gwen-un*
Gwiber	adder, viper	*Goo-iber*
Gwiwer	red squirrel	*Gwee-were*
Gwylan	seagull	*Goo-u-lan*
Hebog	hawk	*Hee-bog*
Hwch	sow; swine	*Hook*

Hydd	stag, hart	*Hee-th*
Llwynog	fox	*Loo-un-og*
Llygoden	mouse	*Lee-god-en*
Lwrch	roebuck	*Loo-erk*
Maharen	ram, wether	*Ma-harren*
March	horse, stallion	*Mark*
Mochyn	pig	*Mock-un*
Neidr	snake	*Neye-der*
Oen	lamb	*Oye-n*
Pi/pia	magpie	*Pee-a*
Soch	pig	*Sock*
Tarw	bull	*Tarroo*
Twrch	wild boar, hog	*Too-erk*
Tylluan	owl	*Tuthl-ee-an*
Wiwer	red squirrel	*Wee-were*
Ych/ychen	ox, oxen	*Uk-en*

Vanished Wildlife

WELSH PLACE NAMES *often refer to now rare or vanished mammals and birds, and give a fascinating glimpse of the wildlife of Wales in the past. Long extinct wolf packs are commemorated in the names Llannerchybleiddiau ('glade of wolves') and Ffosbleiddiad ('ditch of wolves'). The beaver too survives only in name in places such as Llyn yr Afanc ('lake of the beaver') on the river Conwy. Pine martens and otters are rare today but still occur in Craig y Bela ('marten's rock') near Llyn Padarn, and Pont Rhyd y Dyfrgi ('bridge ford of the otter'), near Ysbyty Ifan. Equally interesting are Deri Garan, meaning 'oak trees of the crane', and Cors y Barcud ('marsh of the red kite').*

Picture This: **Names** in the **Landscape**

hillfort ***dinas***

castle ***castell***

mill ***melin***

waterfall ***pistyll***

church ***eglwys***

well ***ffynnon***

bridge ***pont***

island ***ynys***

bare hill ***moel***

river ***afon***

road ***ffordd***

cave ***ogof***

cross *croes*   beach *traeth*   church *llan*

ford *rhyd*   house *tŷ*   stream *nant*

stone *maen*   lake *llyn*   steep slope *llethr*

mountain *mynydd*   chapel *capel*   wood *coed*

Place Names
by Modern County

WALES WAS DIVIDED in 1996 into 22 unitary authorities known collectively as the Principal Areas of Wales. Together, they comprise nine counties, ten county boroughs and three cities. The largest is the so-called 'green desert' of rural Powys in central Wales, and the smallest Blaenau Gwent in the industrialised and more heavily populated south. But although each of the 22 authorities varies considerably in geographical size, all have similar populations and equal status.

In this book, the counties are listed from the north downwards—starting in Anglesey/Ynys Môn and working from left to right, down the map, finishing with Monmouthshire/Mynwy.

"More and more Welsh signs lead to fewer and fewer Welsh places."

Ned Thomas, in *The Welsh Language Today*, 1973

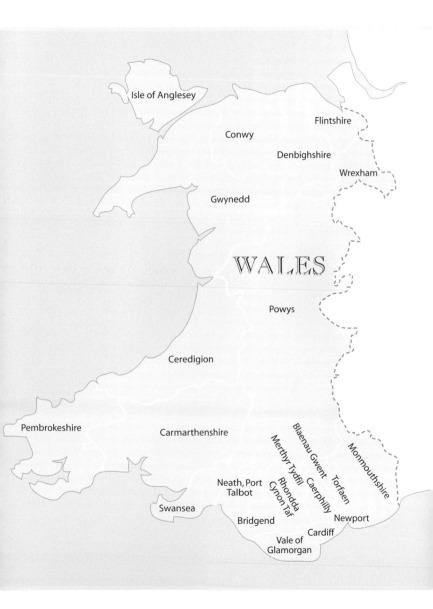

Isle of Anglesey/Ynys Môn

Aberffraw	mouth of the River Ffraw
Afon Alaw	River Alaw (water lilies)
Afon Braint	River Braint (Celtic goddess)
Afon Cefni	River Cefni (rising in a mountain hollow)
Amlwch	around the muddy inlet
Bachau	river bends
Barclodiad y Gawres	apronful of the giantess
Benllech	capstone of the cromlech
Bethel	Bethel chapel (biblical name)
Bodedern	home of Edern (personal name)
Bodewryd	home or church of Gewryd
Bodffordd	home by a ford
Bodorgan	home of Corgyn (personal name)
Bryngwran	hill of Gwran (personal name)
Bryn Du	black hill
Bryn Celli Ddu	hill of the black grove
Brynrefail	hill of the smithy
Brynsiencyn	hill of Siencyn (personal name)
Brynteg	lovely or fair hill
Caergeiliog	fort of Ceiliog (personal name)
Caergybi	(Holyhead) fort of St Cybi
Capel Coch	red chapel
Capel Gwyn	white chapel
Capel Mawr	big chapel
Caergaeliog	fort of the cockerel
Carmel	Carmel chapel (biblical name)
Carreglefn	smooth or slippery rock
Cemaes	river meanders
Cemlyn	curved lake or bay
Cerrigceinwen	rocks of Ceinwen (personal name)
Coedana	St Anaf's wood
Dulas	dark, black stream
Dwyran	two parts
Elim	Elim (biblical name)
Gaerwen	white fort
Glan-yr-afon	bank of the river
Gogarth	low rise in the ground
Gwalchmai	township of Gwalchmai (personal name)
Gwredog	downward slope
Hebron	Hebron chapel (biblical name)
Hen Blas	old or former mansion

Hen Borth	old or former harbour
Heneglwys	old church
Hermon	Hermon chapel (biblical name)
Llanbabo	church of St Pabo
Llanerchymedd	glade of mead [honey beer]
Llanfflewyn	church of St Fflewin
Llangoch	red church
Llanallgo	church of St Gallgov
Llanbadrig	church of St Patrick
Llanddanielfab	church of St Daniel Vab
Llanddona	church of St Dona
Llanddeusant	church of two saints
Llandegfan	church of St Tegfan
Llandyfrydog	church of St Tyfrydog
Llaneilian	church of St Eilian
Llanfachraeth	church of St Machraith
Llanfaelog	church of St Maelog
Llanfaes	church in the open fields

Colours in the Countryside

A SURPRISINGLY SMALL PALETTE *of natural colours dominates the Welsh countryside. Probably the commonest colours found in place names are green (glas/las or gwyrdd), red (coch), black (du/ddu), grey (llwyd) and white (gwyn/ gwen/wen). Good examples of these include: Glasgwm ('green valley'), in Powys; Crib Goch ('red ridge'), in Gwynedd; Ynys Ddu ('black' or 'dark island'), in Monmouthshire; Llwydiarth ('the grey hillside'), in Powys; and Bryn-gwyn ('white' or 'holy hill'), in Anglesey. The Welsh for yellow is melyn, as in Mynydd Melyn ('yellow mountain') in Pembrokeshire. Silver (arian) and gold (aur) occur too, in place names such as Carn yr Arian (the 'silver cairn'), and Llannerch-yr- aur (the 'golden glade'), both in Powys.*

Llanfair-is-gaer	St Mary's church below the fort
Llanfairpwllgwyngyll	St Mary's church of the pool of the white hazels
Llanfair-yn-y-Cwmwd	St Mary's church in the commote of Menai
Llanfairynghornwy	St Mary's church of Cornwy (personal name)
Llanfair-yn-Neubwll	St Mary's church by the two pools
Llanfechell	church of St Mechyll
Llanfihangel-yn-Nhywyn	St Michael's church in the dunes
Llanfwrog	church of St Mwrog
Llangadwaladr	church of Cadwaladr (personal name)
Llangaffo	church of St Caffo
Llangefni	church on the River Cefni
Llangeinwen	church of St Ceinwen
Llangoed	church near the wood
Llangristiolus	church of Cristiolus (personal name)
Llanrhyddlad	church of St Rhyddlad
Llansadwrn	church of Sadwrn (personal name)
Llantrisant	church of three saints
Llanynghenedl	church of St Enghenel
Llechylched	gravestone of St Ilched
Llyn Alaw	lake of waterlilies
Llyn Llywenan	happy lake
Maenaddwyn	stone of Addwyn (personal name)
Malltraeth	unwholesome or fetid beach
Marianglas	grassy rock-strewn land
Menai	narrow water
Moelfre	bare hill
Nebo	Nebo chapel (biblical name)
Niwbwrch	Welsh for 'Newborough'
Pencarnisiog	above Carnisiog
Pengorffwysfa	top of the resting place
Penllin	flax headland
Penmon	tip of Anglesey ('Ynys Mon')
Penrhos	head of the moor
Penrhyn Mawr	big headland
Pentraeth	end of the beach
Pentreberw	village in Berw
Pentrefelin	mill village
Pen-y-garnedd	top of the cairn
Penysarn	end of the causeway
Porth Tywynmawr	harbour of the big sandy beach
Porth Wen	white or fair harbour
Rhos Lligwy	[river] Lligwy moor
Rhosbeirio	St Peirio's moor

Rhoscefnhir	moor of the long ridge
Rhoscolyn	Colyn's headland (personal name)
Rhosgoch	red moor
Rhosmeirch	moor of the stallions
Rhosneigr	Neigr's moor (personal name)
Rhos-y-bol	hummocky moor
Rhydwyn	white or blessed ford
Talwrn	threshing floor, cockpit
Trearddur	Iarddur's settlement (personal name)
Trefdraeth	shore farm or settlement
Trefor	after Trevor Jones, quarry manager
Tregele	leech hamlet
Valley	from Welsh 'mael-dy', house of trade
Wylfa	lookout point
Y Felinheli	the mill of salt water
Ynys Môn	(Isle of Anglesey)

Weapons and Warfare

WALES IS DOTTED WITH REMINDERS *of ancient warfare. From Iron Age tribal battles to Roman, Anglo-Saxon and English incursions and invasions, conflict is reflected in many Welsh place names. Common war-related place name elements include* dinas *meaning a 'safe place' or 'hillfort', and* caer *meaning a 'barred' or 'fortified place'; while* castell *is the Welsh version of the Latin 'castellum'.* Byddin *means a 'troop' or 'army'; and* cad *and* trin *mean a 'battle' or 'army', too. Many place names also contain references to weapons:* saeth *means 'arrow',* gelau *is a 'sword' or 'blade',* gwain *a 'sheath' or 'scabbard', and* ysgwyd *a 'shield'.*

Warrior's head, St Michael's church, Bugeildy, Powys

Did You Know? The Longest Place Name in Wales

AN UNASSUMING VILLAGE alongside the Menai Strait, on the Isle of Anglesey, boasts the longest place name in Britain. **Llanfairpwllgwyngyllgogerchwyrndrobwllllantysiliogogogoch** means: 'St Mary's church in the hollow of white hazels near the rapid whirlpool by St Tysilio's church of the red cave'.

To the English eye, the name is 58 letters long. Yet, because in Welsh 'll' and 'ch' are classed as letters in their own right, the name properly has only 51 letters. Even so, Wales' longest place name has fascinated visitors from across the world for over 150 years, and in Victorian times was fondly nicknamed the 'Great Jawbreaker'.

Until the Chester to Holyhead railway arrived in 1848, the quiet village was known simply as Llanfair Pwllgwyngyll. Then local businessmen, keen to draw in English tourists and their money, devised a cunning plan to rename the new railway station. A local cobbler (or maybe a tailor, depending on which version of the story you choose to believe) from nearby Menai Bridge came up with the 'longest name' idea and, tongue in cheek, cobbled together the necessary extra syllables.

Little did he realise he'd just created one of Europe's finest early tourist marketing schemes.

Today, the village is signposted as Llanfairpwllgwyngyll but is known to locals as Llanfairpwll or plain Llanfair PG. And the old station buildings, which were closed in 1973, were reopened in 1993 as a Welsh weaving shop, visitor centre and café.

Ask nicely in the Visitor Centre and the well-practised staff will (probably) pronounce the name for you.

Victorian souvenir postcard

Llanfairpwllgwyngyllgogerchwyrndrobwllllantysiliogog-ogoch

St Mary's church—in the hollow—of white hazels—near to the rapid whirlpool—by St Tysilio's church—of the red cave

How to say it:
'thlan-vire-pooth-gwinn-gith-gogg-erra-kweern-drobbooth-lan-tuss-ill-yo-goggo-gauk'

The station and its famous sign, Llanfair PG, Isle of Anglesey

Conwy

Abergele	mouth of the river Gele
Afon Aled	river Aled (flow of water)
Afon Conwy	river Conwy (reed river)
Afon Ddu	dark or black river
Afon Derfyn	river Derfyn (boundary)
Afon Dulyn	river Dulyn
Bae Colwyn	(Colwyn Bay) bay of the river Colwyn
Betws-y-Coed	prayer house in the woods
Betws-yn-Rhos	prayer house in the moors
Bodnant	home of note
Bryn-y-Maen	hill of stone
Bwlch Gwyn	white pass
Bylchau	gaps or passes
Caer Caradog	Caradog's stronghold (personal name)
Caernarfon	fortress facing Anglesey
Capel Curig	chapel of Curig (personal name)
Capel Garmon	chapel of Garmon (personal name)
Capelulo	chapel of Ulo (personal name)
Carnedd Dafydd	cairn of Dafydd (personal name)
Carnedd Llewelyn	cairn of Llewelyn (personal name)
Castell Cawr	giant's castle
Cefn-brith	speckled ridge
Cefn-coch	red ridge
Cefn Llysgwr	ridge by a gentleman's mansion
Cerrigydrudion	stones of the brave warriors or heroes
Colwyn	puppy, cub
Conwy	(Conway) Conwy river
Dawn	moor of the sons-in-law
Deganwy	land of the tribe of Decanae
Dolgarrog	meadow of the swift flowing stream
Dolwen	fair meadow
Dolwyddelan	meadow of Gwyddelan (personal name)
Dwygyfylchi	two round forts
Eglwysbach	church in a nook
Gell	place near the river Gell
Glan Conwy	bank of the river Conwy
Glasfryn	green or fresh hill
Glyder Fach	little heap
Glyder Fawr	big heap
Gwarthaf	upper hundred

Gwytherin	Gwytherin's place (personal name)
Hafod Dinbych	summer dwelling of the little fort
Henryd	old ford
Llanbedr-y-Cennin	St Peter's church by the leek field
Llanddoged	church of St Doged
Llanddulas	church of the river Dulas (dark water)
Llandrillo-yn-Rhos	church of St Trillo on the moor
Llandudno	church of St Tudno
Llaneilian-yn-Rhos	church of St Elian on the moor
Llanfair Talhaiarn	St Mary's church of Talhaern (personal name)
Llanfairfechan	lesser church of St Mary's
Llanfihangel Glyn Myfyr	St Michael's church in the valley of Myfyr (pers. name)
Llangernyw	church of Cernyw (personal name)
Llangwm	church in the valley
Llanrhychwyn	church of St Rhychwyn
Llanrwst	church of St Gwrwst (personal name)
Llansanffraid Glan Conwy	church of St Bridget in the Conwy valley
Llansannan	church of Sannan (personal name)

Forts and Castles

DEFENDED SETTLEMENTS, *hillforts and castles are common across Wales. Some of the earliest fortified places were Iron Age hillforts dominating the high places.* Din *and* dinas *both mean a 'fortified hill', 'fort' or 'stronghold', while* dinlle *means the 'site of a fort' or 'land around a defended settlement'. Examples include* Dinas Mawddwy *('fort of Mawddwy') in Gwynedd, and* Dinbych/Denbigh *('little fortress') in Denbighshire. Similarly,* caer *means an 'enclosed or fortified place', as in* Caerdydd/Cardiff *('fortress on the river Taf'), or* Caernarfon *('fortress in Arfon'). Finally,* castell *is the Welsh for castle—as in* Castell Dinas Bran *('castle fort of the raven'), above Llangollen, in North Wales.*

Llyn Aled	lake Aled (personal name)
Llyn Alwen	lake Alwen
Llyn Brenig	lake of the river Brenig (limpets)
Llyn Cowlyd	lake of Cowlyd
Llyn Crafnant	lake of the stream of wild garlic/ramsons
Llyn Eigiau	lake of shoals of fish
Llyn Ogwen	lake of the lively piglet
Llysfaen	stone court
Maenan	little stone
Melin-y-coed	mill wood
Migneint	marshy streams
Mochdre	pig farmstead
Moel Llyn	bare hill of the lake
Moel Siabod	bare scabby hill
Nebo	Nebo chapel (biblical name)
Pandy Tudur	dirty or muddy fulling mill
Penmachno	head of the valley of Machno (personal name)

River Goddesses

RIVERS, LAKES AND SPRINGS *were sacred to the early Celtic tribes of Wales who believed water was the home of spirits. Welsh river names have changed surprisingly little over thousands of years, and many still reflect the names of ancient gods and goddesses. To please these powerful deities, the Celts sometimes cast jewellery or weapons into the water as votive offerings. The River Dee, or Afon Dyfrdwy, in North Wales takes its name from the words* dwfr *('water') and* dwy *(meaning 'goddess'). Similarly, both the Afon Dwyfor and Afon Dwyfach, in Gwynedd, are named after river goddesses. More specifically, Afon Aeron, in Ceredigion, celebrates Aerfen, the Celtic goddess of war.*

"All Wales is a sea of song"

Owen M Edwards, *Adfyfyrion,* 1907

Penmaen-mawr	head of the big rock
Pensarn	end of the road or paved way
Pentrefoelas	village of the bare green hill
Pentre-tafarn-y-fedw	village near the birch tree tavern
Rhos-y-mawn	peat moor
Rowen	place of white pebbles
Rhydlydan	broad ford
Rhyd-y-foel	ford by the hilltop
Tal-y-bont	front of the bridge
Tal-y-cafn	ferry boat end
Tal-y-Fan	top of the peak
Tywyn	sand dune
Trefriw	settlement of the hillside
Trofarth	slope in the wheel hub
Tŷ Nant	house of the stream
Tŷ'n-y-Groes	house of the crossroads
Y Tryfan	the rounded peak
Ysbyty Ifan	hospital or almshouses of Ifan (personal name)

Denbighshire/Dinbych

Aberchwiler	mouth of the river Chwiler
Afon Alun	river Alyn (personal name)
Afon Clwyd	river Clwyd (hurdle fence across the river)
Afon Morynion	river of the maids
Aifft	Egypt
Berwyn	white topped mountain
Betws Gwerful Goch	prayer house of Gwerful the Red
Bodelwyddan	home of Elwyddan (personal name)
Bodfari	church of St Barre or St Deufaru
Bontuchel	high bridge
Brynsaithmarchog	St Marchog/Marchan's hill
Bryneglwys	hill of the church
Bylchau	gaps or passes
Cadair Berwyn	seat or stronghold of the snow tops
Cadair Fronwen	seat or stronghold of Bronwen
Carrog	swift flowing stream
Castell	castle
Cefnmeriadog	St Meriadog's ridge
Clawdd newydd	new bank
Clocaenog	knoll of lichen
Corwen	sanctuary stone
Crogen	shell
Cwm	valley
Cyfeiliog	Cyfael's land
Cyrn-y-brain	cairn of the ravens
Cynwyd	St Cynwyd
Dinbych	(Denbigh) small safe place or city
Derwen	oak tree
Dregoch	red settlement
Dwyryd	(Druid) two fords
Dyserth	wilderness
Efenechtyd	the monastery or grange
Eryrys	flock of eagles
Ffordd Las	green way
Fridd Fawr	large upland pasture
Froncysyllte	hillside of joining or linking
Gallt Melyd	hill of Melyd (personal name)
Garth	wooded ridge or yard/enclosure
Gellifor	big grove

Gellïoedd	groves
Glasfryn	green hill
Glyndyfrdwy	glen of the river Dyfrdwy (water goddess)
Graig	rock
Graig Fawr	great rock
Graig-fechan	little rock
Groes	the cross
Gronant	shingle stream
Gwaenysgor	field with a yard
Gwyddelwern	thicket on the marshland
Henllan	old or former church
Hiraethog	long mountain of gorse
Hirwaen	long meadow
Lawnt	lawn
Llanarmon-yn-Iâl	church of Garmon in Iâl (Yale)
Llanasa	church of St Asa
Llanbedr-Dyffryn-Clwyd	church of St Peter in the valley of the river Clwyd

Streams and Rivers

WELSH RIVER NAMES *are often descriptive and provide useful clues to their character. Calm or gently flowing waters are suggested by names such as Afon Honddu (from the Welsh* hawdd, *meaning 'easy' or 'leisurely') and Afon Llyfni (from* llyfni *meaning 'smooth'). In contrast, the name Afon Garw comes from* garw *(meaning 'rough' or 'rugged') suggesting a wilder stream. Other river names reflect the noise of running water, as in Afon Clywedog ('noisy'), Afon Llafar ('babbling' or 'vocal') or, conversely, its silence, as in Afon Tawe (from* tawel, *meaning 'quiet').*

Afon Tawe, near Swansea

Llandegla	church of St Tecla
Llannefydd	church of St Ufydd
Llanelidan	church of St Elidan
Llandrillo	church of St Trillo
Llandyrnog	church of St Tyrnog
Llanelwy	church on the river Elwy (St Asaph)
Llanfair Dyffryn Clwyd	church of St Mary in the valley of the Clwyd
Llanferres	church of St Berrys
Llanfwrog	church of Mwrog (personal name)
Llangollen	church of St Collen
Llangwm	church in the valley
Llangwyfan	church of St Cwyfan
Llangyhafal	church of St Cynhafal
Llanrhaeadr	church by the waterfall
Llansannan	church of the little saint
Llantysilio	church of St Tysilio
Llanynys	church of the island
Llwyn	grove
Llyn Brenig	lake of the river Brenig (limpets)
Marian Cwm	valley of the moraine
Meliden	hill of St Melydn
Melin-y-wig	mill of the clearing
Moel Arthur	Arthur's bare hill
Moel Eithinen	bare hill of gorse
Moel Famau	bare hill of Mama (personal name)
Moel Maenefa	bare hill of Eve's stone
Moel Hiraddug	bare hill of the long attack
Moel y Gamelin	bare hill of the crooked elbow
Myneddllech	mountain slab
Nantferres	stream or valley of Berres (personal name)
Nantglyn	stream in the valley
Pentre Llanrhaeadr	village of the church of the waterfall
Pentre-celyn	Cuhelyn's settlement'(personal name)
Pentre-dŵr	village of the water
Pen-y-stryt	end of the street
Pontcysyllte	hillside of the joining
Pontystrad	bridge in the vale
Prestatyn	priests' farm
Prion	perfection
Pwll-glas	green or verdant pool
Rhewl	from 'yr heol', the paved road

Rhiwbebyll	hill of tents
Rhuallt	steep hill
Rhuddlan	red bank
Rhuthun	red fort on the bank
Rhyl	Welsh version of the English name 'The Hill'
Saron	Saron chapel (biblical name)
Sodom	Sodom chapel (biblical name)
Tafarn y Gelyn	the Holly Inn
Trefnant	settlement on the stream
Trelawnyd	Llyfynwyd's settlement (personal name)
Tremeirchion	settlement of Meirchion (personal name)
Ty'n-dŵr	smallholding of the water
Waen	the marshland
Y Gyffylliog	the place of pollarded trees
Y Maerdy	the dairy or steward's house

Wild Water?

IN THE CELTIC IMAGINATION, *rivers were often thought to resemble sacred animals. There are rivers named after horses, bulls, boars, cubs, puppies and other creatures across Wales. Marchnant means 'horse stream', and Afon Caseg 'mare river'. Nantybwla means 'bull stream'. Pig names are common, too. Afon Twrch ('boar river') furrows its way through the earth like a pig, as do Afon Hwch ('sow river'), and Afon Banw ('piglets river'). Similarly, the fast, gambolling Afon Colwyn ('young dog' or 'cub') conjures up an image of a playful puppy splashing in the shallows.*

Flintshire/Fflint

Alltami	on or opposite the hillside
Bagillt	from Old English 'Backelie', or 'Bacca's clearing'
Cadole	from the English 'cat hole'
Caergwrle	fort by the heron's meadow
Caerwys	fair fort
Carmel	Mount Carmel (biblical name)
Cilcain	pleasant retreat
Coed Talon	trees around the clearing
Ewloe	from the Old English, 'hill at the source of a stream'
Ffrith	mountain pasture
Ffynnongroyw	clear well or spring
Fflint	from the Latin *castellum-super-fluentum*, 'castle by the sea'
Glan-y-don	shore of the wave
Gorsedd	tumulus or burial mound
Gronant	pebbly stream
Gwaunysgor	meadow by the fort
Gwernaffield	alder-grove field
Gwernymynydd	alder-grove of the mountain
Gwespyr	lookout fort
Halkyn	cavities or mine shafts
Lixwm	from the English, 'likesome' or 'pleasant'
Llanasa	church of Asa (personal name)
Lloc	shelter, sheepfold
Moel-y-Crio	bare hill of the holes
Mostyn	marsh farm
Nannerch	dappled stream
Nercwys	at the dappled stream
Pantasaph	hollow of St Asaph (personal name)
Pant-y-mwyn	hollow of the mine
Pen-y-felin	top of the mill
Pontybotgin	bridge at the bodkin [or borer]
Rhes-y-cae	row [of houses] beside the field
Sychdyn	from the Old English 'bog farm'
Trelawnyd	home of Lawnyd (personal name)
Trelogan	farm at the river Helogan
Ysceifiog	sloping place

Wrexham/Wrecsam

Bwlch-gwyn	white or fair pass
Bangor-is-y-coed	prayer house below the trees
Cefn-mawr	big ridge
Coed-poeth	burnt or hot wood
Gwersyllt	hill of Wersige (personal name)
Llay	from the Old English word for a 'river meadow'
Marchwiel	big saplings
Minera	mine
Pen-y-cae	top of the field
Rhosllannerchrugog	moorland of the heathery glade
Rhostyllen	moorland on a ledge
Rhosymedre	capability moor
Rossett	(from Yr Orsedd) the red mound
Rhiwabon	(Ruabon) hillside of St Mabon
Trefor	big settlement
Y Waun	(Chirk) the moor

Waterfalls

IN A LAND OF MOUNTAINS AND RAIN, *waterfalls are part of the landscape. Welsh uses several words to describe them. In the north* rhaeadr, *and in the south* sgwd *or* ysgwd, *refer to substantial waterfalls; while* pistyll *means a smaller fall, spout or cataract. Places named after waterfalls include Pistyll Rhaeadr—Wales' highest waterfall, and one of the 'Seven Wonders of Wales'—near Llanrhaeadr ym Mochnant, in Denbighshire, and the town of Rhayader (or Rhaeadr Gwy, 'waterfall on the river Wye'), in Powys. Other important Welsh waterfalls include the Aber Falls (Rhaeadr Fawr or 'great falls'), near Abergwyngregyn in Gwynedd, and the Swallow Falls (Rhaeadr Ewynnol or 'foaming waterfall'), between Capel Curig and Betws-y-coed, in Conwy.*

Did You Know?
How Snowdon/Yr Wyddfa
Got Its Name

I T's NO COINCIDENCE that both the English and Welsh names for Wales' highest mountain—Snowdon and Yr Wyddfa—refer to its prominence and visibility from afar. They suggest that for many centuries Snowdon and the surrounding peaks were white with snow throughout the year.

The English name, Snowdon, comes from two Old English (or Saxon) words *snaw* ('snow') and *dun* ('hill' or 'fort'), meaning something like 'the snowy stronghold'. Similarly, its Welsh name, Yr Wyddfa, derives from the two Welsh elements *gwydd* (meaning 'in sight' or 'prominent') and *ma* (or 'place'). The composite word *gwyddfa* later came to mean a 'memorial cairn' or 'burial mound', probably because these ancient monuments to the illustrious dead were usually built on prominent hilltops.

Yr Wyddfa is often translated as 'the burial cairn' and linked to Rhita Fawr, a legendary giantess said to be buried beneath a cairn ('Gwyddfa Rhita') on the summit. According to the story, she was killed by King Arthur, who fought his last battle, and died, at Bwlch y Saethau (the 'pass of arrows') just below the top of the mountain.

Today, Snowdon's summit is crowned by a cairn and the new café and visitor centre called Hafod Eryri ('Snowdonia summer house'). On it is carved this couplet by the Welsh National Poet, Gwyn Thomas: 'Copa'r Wyddfa :yr ydych chwi yma, yn nes at y nefoedd'.

Which means, in English: '*The summit of Snowdon: you are here, nearer to heaven.*'

Snowdon from Llynnau Mymbyr, Gwynedd

Gwynedd

Aberangell	mouth of the river Angell (tributary)
Aberdaron	mouth of the river Daron
Aberdyfi	mouth of the river Dyfi
Abererch	mouth of the river Erch (speckled)
Abergwyngregyn	river mouth of white shells
Abergynolwyn	mouth of the river Gynolwyn (personal name)
Aberllefenni	mouth of the river Llefenni (elm trees)
Abersoch	mouth of the river Soch
Afon Caseg	mare river
Afon Dyfi	dark river
Afon Dysynni	boundary river
Afon Gain	gleaming river
Afon Gamlan	meandering river
Afon Lliw	bright river
Afon Mawddach	little Mawdd river
Afon Tryweryn	river through wetland
Afon Wen	white river
Afon Ysgethin	wild-water river
Aran Fawddwy	little ridge in Mawddwy
Ardudwy	land of the Ardud (tribal name)
Arennig Fawr	big hillside or ridge
Bala	[route] between two lakes
Bangor	wattled fence; enclosure; prayer house
Beddgelert	grave of Saint Celert
Bethel	Bethel chapel (biblical name)
Bethesda	Bethesda chapel (biblical name)
Blaenau Ffestiniog	heads of the valleys in the land of Ffestin
Bodfuan	home of Buan (personal name)
Bontnewydd	new bridge
Borth-y-Gest	harbour of the paunch or belly
Botwnnog	home of Tywynnog (personal name)
Brithdir	mottled land [dotted with stones]
Bryn Mawr	big hill
Bryncir	hill of deer
Bryncrug	hill of the cairn
Brynrefail	hill of the smithy
Bwlchtocyn	pass of the heap or mound
Cadair Idris	seat or stronghold of Idris
Caeathro	teacher's field
Carmel	Carmel chapel (biblical name)
Ceunant	stream gorge

Chwilog	place of insects
Clynnog-fawr	greater holly trees
Corris Uchaf	upper little one [river]
Criccieth	cairn of captives
Croesor	many crosses
Cwm-y-Glo	valley of coal
Deiniolen	Deiniolen's settlement (personal name)
Diffwys	wilderness; steep slope
Dinas Mawddwy	fort of Mawddwy (personal name)
Dinorwig	(possibly) fort of the Ordovices tribe
Dolbenmaen	meadow at the top of the rock
Dolgellau	meadow of monk's cells
Edern	[church of] Edern (personal name)
Efailnewydd	new smithy
Ffestiniog	land of Ffestin (personal name)
Fron-goch	red hillside
Ganllwyd	the shaded [lively] white horse [river]
Garn Dolbenmaen	cairn of the meadow at the top of the rock

Watermills and Windmills

BEFORE THE INDUSTRIAL REVOLUTION, *Welsh mills were powered by wind or water. The Welsh word for mill is* melin; *so a watermill is* melin dŵr *and a windmill* melin gwynt, *or* melinwynt. *Watermills harnessed a river or stream, or occasionally the tidal flow of an estuary, to grind the corn or process woollen cloth. The grain for the mills was stored in barns; places named after them include Ysgubor-fawr or the 'great barn', and Ysguboriau or 'barns'—both in Pembrokeshire. A fulling mill, used to beat and finish woollen cloth, has a different name and is called a* pandy, *as in Pandy Tudur ('dirty fulling mill'), in Conwy, and Tonypandy ('meadow of the fulling mill'), in Rhondda Cynon Taf.*

Garreg	rock or stone
Gellilydan	broad grove
Glasinfryn	green or fresh hill
Golan	Golan chapel (biblical name)
Harlech	beautiful slab or rock
Llanaelhaearn	church of St Aelhaiarn
Llanbedr	church of St Peter
Llanbedrog	church of Pedrog (personal name)
Llandanwg	church of Tanwg (personal name)
Llanddeiniolen	church of Deiniol (personal name)
Llandderfel	church of Derfael (personal name)
Llandudwen	church of St Tudwen
Llandwrog	church of St Twrog
Llandygai	church of St Tygai
Llanegryn	church of Egryn (personal name)
Llanelltyd	church of St Elltud
Llanenddwyn	church of Enddwyn (personal name)
Llanengan	church of Einion (personal name)
Llanfachraeth	church of Machraith (personal name)
Llanfair	church of St Mary
Llanfihangel-y-traethau	church of St Mary of the beaches
Llanfor	big church
Llangelynnin	church of Celynnin (personal name)
Llangian	church of St Cian
Llangywer	church of St Cywair
Llangwnadl	nant (valley) of Gwyn Hoedl (personal name)
Llangybi	church of Cybi (personal name)
Llaniestyn	church of St Iestyn
Llanllechid	church of Llechid (personal name)
Llanllyfni	church beside the river Llynfi
Llannor	big church
Llanrug	church in the heather
Llanuwchllyn	church above the lake
Llanwnda	church of St Gwndaf
Llanymawddwy	church in Mawddwy
Llanystumdwy	church on the bend of the river Dwy
Llithfaen	lodestone
Llwyngwril	grove of Gwril (personal name)
Llyn Arenig Fawr	lake of Arenig Fawr mountain
Llyn Celyn	holly lake
Llyn Cwellyn	fish trap lake
Llyn Gwynant	lake in a fair valley
Llyn Llydaw	lakeside

Llyn Padarn	lake at Dolbadarn
Llyn Peris	lake of St Peris
Llyn Tegid	lake of Tegid (personal name)
Maentwrog	stone of Twrog (personal name)
Minffordd	roadside
Minllyn	lakeshore
Moel Ddu	bare black hill
Moel Eilio	bare hill of Eilio (personal name)
Moel Hebog	bare hill of the hawk
Moel Wnion	bare hill of Gwynion (personal name)
Moel Ysgyfarnogod	bare hill of hares
Moelwyn Bach	little bare hill
Moelwyn Mawr	big bare hill
Moel-y-Geifr	bare hill of goats
Morfa Nefyn	sea marsh of Nefyn (personal name)
Nant Peris	St Peris' valley
Nantmor	big stream
Nasareth	Nazareth chapel (biblical name)

Fords, Ferries and Bridges

WELSH RIVERS AND STREAMS *were often real obstacles to early travellers. They were thought to be the home of wilful spirits and could be difficult or dangerous to cross. So the first fords, ferries and bridges were important places, often with distinctive names. The Welsh for ford is rhyd. Fords were once far more common than today and occur widely in place names such as Rhyd-ddu ('dark ford'), in Gwynedd, and Rhyd-y-wrach ('the witch's ford'), in Carmarthenshire. The Welsh for a boat or ferry is ysgraff or bad, as in Ceubalfa ('ferry boat place'), in Powys, and Gabalfa, in Cardiff. Most common of all, though, are places named after a bridge (pont or bont), such as Pont-faen ('stone bridge') in Pembrokeshire, and Pontnewydd ('new bridge') in Monmouthshire.*

Stepping stones, near Newborough, Isle of Anglesey

Nebo	Nebo chapel (biblical name)
Nefyn	[place of] Nevin (personal name)
Pant Glas	green or verdant hollow
Parc	park
Penmaenpool	pool by the prominent rock
Penmorfa	end of the sea marsh
Pennal	head of the moor
Penrhos	head of the moorland
Penrhyndeudraeth	headland of two beaches
Pentir	headland
Pentrefelin	village of the mill
Pen-y-graig	head of the rock
Penygroes	head of the crossroads
Pistyll	waterfall
Porth Ceiriad	Ceiriad's bay (personal name)
Porth Colwyn	pup's cove
Porth Golman	Golman's cove (personal name)
Porth Nefyn	harbour of Nefyn (personal name)
Porth Ysgaden	herring cove
Porthmadog	Madock's harbour
Porthoer	cold harbour
Prenteg	fine tree
Pwllheli	pool of salt water
Rachub	the holding
Rhinog Fawr	great threshold
Rhiwlas	green hillside
Rhobell Fawr	big saddle-shaped ridge
Rhoshirwaun	moorland of the long pasture
Rhoslefain	flat moor
Rhostryfan	moorland of the rounded summit
Rhos-y-gwaliau	moorland near the walls (of Plas Rhiwaedog)
Rhyd	ford or river crossing
Rhyd-y-clafdy	ford or river crossing by the leper house
Rhydygroes	ford or river crossing by the cross
Ro-wen	place of white pebbles
Salem	Salem chapel (biblical name)
Sarn	paved way, road
Saron	Saron chapel (biblical name)
Seion	Zion chapel (biblical name)
Snowdon	see Yr Wyddfa
Talsarnau	end of the paved roads
Tal-y-bont	end of the bridge

Tal-y-llyn	end of the lake
Talysarn	end of the paved road
Tanygrisiau	below the steps
Trawsfynydd	across the mountain
Trefor	large settlement
Tregarth	settlement of the enclosure
Tremadog	settlement of Madog (personal name)
Tudweiliog	place of St Tudwal (personal name)
Tywyn	sandy beach, shore
Waun Oer	cold mountain pasture
Waunfawr	big mountain pasture
Y Drum	the summit
Y Dduallt	the dark wooded hillside
Y Llethr	the slope
Y Rhiw	the hillside
Ynys Enlli	(Bardsey) Enlli's island (personal name)
Yr Eifl	the gap of two peaks
Yr Wyddfa	(Snowdon) the memorial cairn

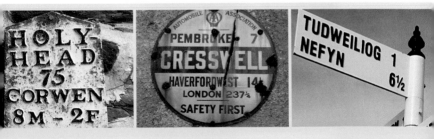

On the Road

TRACKS AND LONG-DISTANCE TRADE ROUTES *have criss-crossed Wales since prehistoric times. But the first real roads were Roman—often described by the Welsh word* sarn, *meaning a paved way. Surviving stretches of Sarn Helen, the longest Roman road in Wales, can still be traced between Aberconwy in North Wales and Carmarthen in the south. Other Welsh words for a road include* heol *and* ffordd, *as in Heolgerrig (or 'stone road') in Merthyr Tydfil, and Ffordd Saeson ('Englishman's road'), in Denbighshire.* Bwlch *means a 'mountain pass' or 'gap', adwy a 'breach' or 'gap', and* drws *a 'doorway' or 'pass'—for example Adwy'r Clawdd ('gap in the [Offa's] dyke, in Wrexham; and Bwlch y Oerddrws ('pass of the cold doorway'), in Gwynedd.*

Did You Know? The Legend of Gelert's Grave

Beddgelert in the heart of Snowdonia
Above: Hand-carved slate gravestones in English and Welsh

B EDDGELERT IS A PICTURESQUE mountain village just south of Snowdon, in the heart of the Snowdonia National Park. It's a popular tourist 'honey-pot' whose main claim to fame is the riverside Gelert's Grave. Two slate memorials on a cairn of stones—one in English and one in Welsh—tell the bitter-sweet tale of Gelert the faithful hound. But is the Beddgelert story a genuine account of a historic tragedy, or simply the cunning concoction of a Georgian hotelier keen to profit from increasing trade?

The name of the village certainly means 'Gelert's grave' (*bedd* + *Celert*). But there are two conflicting interpretations of the story behind the name. The earliest record of Beddgelert appears in 1258 as *Bekelert*, and today experts suggest the village is probably named after an 8th-century Christian missionary called Saint Celert.

However, the ever-popular romantic version of the tale carved into the gravestones insists:

"In the 13th century, Llewelyn, Prince of North Wales, had a palace at Beddgelert. One day he went hunting without Gelert, 'the faithful hound', who was unaccountably absent. On Llewelyn's return the truant hound, stained and smeared with blood, joyfully sprang to meet his master. The Prince, alarmed, hastened to find his son and saw the infant's cot empty, the bedclothes and floor covered with blood. The frantic father plunged his sword into the hound's side, thinking it had killed his heir. The dog's dying yell was answered by a child's cry. Llewelyn searched and discovered his boy unharmed, but nearby lay the body of a mighty wolf which Gelert had slain. The Prince, filled with remorse, is said never to have smiled again. He buried Gelert here. The spot is called Beddgellert."

A nice story. But probably untrue. In fact, it's a reworking of a well-known folk tale that appears, amongst other places, in the ancient Welsh Mabinogion. It seems the tale of Gelert's Grave and the actual burial mound were created in 1803 by David Pritchard, the landlord of the Beddgelert (now the Royal Goat) Hotel, along with several other local businessmen, to attract the growing number of artists and tourists visiting Wales during the Napoleonic wars.

As an early marketing ploy, it was a brilliant success. And it's still working today.

Ceredigion

Aberaeron	mouth of the river Aeron (goddess of war)
Aberarth	mouth of the river Arth (bear)
Aberporth	mouth of the river harbour
Aberystwyth	mouth of river Ystwyth (winding)
Afon Aeron	river Aeron (goddess of war)
Afon Doethie	river Doethie
Afon Dyfi	dark river
Afon Efyrnwy	Ebur's river (personal name)
Afon Elan	rushing river
Afon Rheidol	quick river
Afon Teifi	dark river
Betws Bledrws	prayer house of Bledrws (personal name)
Betws Ifan	prayer house of Evan (personal name)
Beulah	Beulah chapel (biblical name)
Blaenannerch	source of the river Annerch
Blaenpennal	source of the river Pennal
Blaenplwyf	far end of the parish
Blaenporth	river source by the port
Bontnewydd	new bridge
Borth	harbour
Brongest	belly-like rounded hillside
Brynhoffnant	hillside by the summer stream
Bwlch-llan	pass of the church
Caerwedros	Gwedros's fort (personal name)
Capel Bangor	chapel of the wattle fence
Capel Dewi	chapel of St David
Capel Seion	chapel of Zion (biblical name)
Cardigan	territory of Ceredig
Cefn Cnwc	ridge of the hillock
Cefn Croes	ridge of the cross
Ceinewydd	(Newquay) new quay
Cenarth	lichen ridge
Cilcennin	source of the river Cennin
Cnwch Coch	little red hillock
Cors Caron	bog of Caron (personal name)
Cribyn	crest
Croes-lan	parish crossroads
Cwm Cou	enclosed valley
Cwmsychbant	valley of the dry hollow
Cwmystwyth	valley of the river Ystwyth
Cwrt-Newydd	new court

Dibyn Du	black cliff
Dihewyd	pleasant place
Drum	ridge or summit
Ffair Rhos	moorland fair
Ffostrasol	crowbar ditch
Garth Penrhyngoch	escarpment at the head of the red hill
Glandyfi	bank of the river Dyfi (black water)
Glynarthen	glen of the Arthen brook
Goginan	little ridge
Gorsgoch	red marsh
Hawen	stream that is dry in summer
Llanilar	church of St Ilar
Llanafan	church of St Afan
Llanbedr Pont Steffan	(Lampeter) church of St Peter, bridge of Steven
Llanddeiniol	church of St Deiniol
Llanddewi Brefi	church of St David on the stream
Llandre	church village
Llandygwydd	church of Tygwy (personal name)

Inns and Taverns

MOST OF WALES' OLDEST PUBS *started out as roadside rest and refreshment stops for drovers and other weary travellers. The earliest were simply farmhouses where ale brewed on the premises could be drunk in the kitchen. Many also offered food, games and a bed for the night. It was traditional in Wales to mark a tavern, or* tafarn*, by an evergreen tree or a sheaf of holly beside the door. Tafarngelyn ('holly tavern'), in Denbighshire, and Tafarnyfedw ('birches tavern'), in Conwy, reflect this custom. Today, both are the names of villages that grew up around the original tavern.*

Llandysul	church of St Tysul
Llanfair Clydogau	church of St Mary at the Clywedog rivers
Llanfarian	church of the shingle bank or moraine
Llanfihangel-y-Creuddyn	St Michael's church in Creuddyn
Llangeitho	church of Ceitho (personal name)
Llangrannog	church of Crannog (personal name)
Llangwyryfon	church of the virgins
Llangybi	church of Cybi (personal name)
Llanina	church of St Ina
Llannon	church of Non (personal name)
Llanrhystud	church of Rhystud (personal name)
Llansanffraid	church of St Bridget
Llanwenog	church of St Gwenog
Llanwnnen	church of St Gwynnen
Llan-y-bydder	church of the [once] deaf [to Christ's word]
Llechryd	stone ford [stepping stones]
Lledrod	half shield [semi-circular enclosure]
Llwyncelyn	holly grove
Llwyndafydd	grove of Dafydd (personal name)
Llyn Berwyn	lake of the river Berwyn (foaming)
Llyn Brianne	lake on the river Brianne
Maen-y-Groes	stone of the cross or crossroads
Maesllyn	meadow by the lake
Mydroilin	confluence of river Mydr and Eilin stream
Nanternis	valley of Ernis (personal name)
Nebo	Nebo chapel (biblical)
Pen Bont Rhydybeddau	ridge end at the ford of the graves
Pen Carreg-Gopa	top of the rock crest
Penbryn	top of the hill
Penparc	top of the parkland
Penrhiwllan	church summit
Pentregat	[turnpike] gate village
Plwmp	water pump
Pontgarreg	bridge of stone
Ponthirwaun	bridge of the long moorland
Pontrhydfendigaid	bridge of the ford of the blessed
Pontrhydygroes	bridge of the ford of the cross
Pont Siân	Sian's bridge
Pren-gwyn	white tree
Pumlumon Fawr	big five peaks
Rhydlewis	Lewis's ford (personal name)
Rhydowen	Owain's ford

Rhyd-y-pennau	ford of the hilltops
Salem	Salem chapel (biblical name)
Sarnau	paved ways, roads
Talgarreg	end of the rock
Talsarn	end of the road
Tan-y-groes	below the crossroads
Traeth-saith	beach of the river Saith
Tre Taliesin	home of Talicsin (personal name)
Trefilan	Ilan's farm (personal name)
Tregaron	town or home of Caron (personal name)
Tregroes	settlement at the crossroads
Tremain	stones settlement
Troed-yr-aur	Treyr's farm (personal name)
Tyn-y-graig	croft of the rock
Y Ferwig	the outlying farm
Ynys Lochdyn	island of the fortified inlet
Ysbyty Ystwyth	hospice near the river Ystwyth
Ystrad Aeron	vale of Aeron (goddess of battle)
Ystrad Meurig	vale of Meurig (personal name)

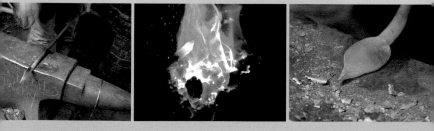

Smiths and Smithies

EVER SINCE THE DISCOVERY OF IRON WORKING *in Britain around 500BC, smiths have been important providers of both everyday tools and weapons of war. In prehistoric times they enjoyed almost magical status—as seen in the megalithic burial chamber at Cerrig-y-Gof ('stones of the smith'), in Pembrokeshire. The Welsh word for a smith is* gof, *as seen, too, in Bron-y-gof ('blacksmith's hill'), in Denbighshire; while a smithy is* efail, *as in Tonyrefail ('smithy meadow'), in Rhondda Cynon Taf. Charcoal for smelting and heating iron was probably produced in Coed y Gof ('smith's wood'), in Gwynedd, and Coedpoeth ('hot' or 'burnt wood'), in Wrexham; while Nant-y-glo ('coal stream valley'), in Blaenau Gwent, reflects the later use of coal.*

Powys

Abbeycwmhir	abbey in the long valley
Abercegir	mouth of the river Cegyr (hemlock)
Aber-craf	mouth of the river Craf (wild garlic)
Aberedw	mouth of the river Edw
Abergwesyn	mouth of the river Gweswyn
Aberhafesb	confluence of the rivers Hafesb and Severn
Aberllynfi	mouth of the river Llynfi (smooth)
Aber-miwl	mouth of the river Miwl
Abertridwr	confluence of three streams
Aberhonddu	(Brecon) mouth of the river Honddu (pleasant)
Adfa	exit route; way to drive animals
Afon Banw	piglet river
Afon Carno	cairn edged river
Afon Hepste	dark river that dries up
Afon Honddu	quiet or pleasant river
Afon Irfon	river Irfon (pre-Celtic personal name?)
Afon Ithon	clamorous river
Afon Senni	Sannon's river (personal name)
Afon Tanat	sparkling river
Afon Tawe	dark or flowing river
Afon Twrch	wild boar river
Afon Twymyn	river of warm water
Afon Wysg	(Usk) fish filled river
Afon Efyrnwy	(Vyrnwy) river Efyrnwy
Banc-y-Celyn	holly bank
Berriew	mouth of the river Rhiw (from aber rhiw)
Betws Cedewain	chapel in the commote of Cedewain
Beulah	Beulah chapel (biblical name)
Blaenllyfni	source of the river Llynfi
Bleddfa	wolf cub's lair
Bont-Dolgadfan	bridge of Cadfan's meadow
Brecon	English name for Aberhonddu
Bronllys	Brwyn's court (personal name)
Bryn	hill
Bryn Amlwg	clearly-seen hill
Bryn Beili	hill of the enclosure
Bryn Bugeiliad	hill of shepherds
Bryn Du	black hill
Bryn Eithinog	hill of gorse
Bryngwyn	white hill
Bwlch	mountain pass

Bugeildy	house of the shepherd
Bwlch-y-cibau	pass of husks or cuplike hollows
Bwlch-y-fridd	sheepwalk pass
Bwlch-y-sarnau	pass of the paved ways
Cadair Berwyn	Berwyn's seat or fort
Caersws	fort of Sws (personal name)
Carcwm	fast-flowing stream valley
Carnedd Wen	white cairn
Carneddau	cairns
Carno	place of cairns
Carreg Goch	red rock
Cefn Clawdd	ridge of the bank
Cefn Coch	red ridge
Cefn Crin	dry ridge
Cefn Crug	ridge of the cairn
Cefn Gwyntog	windy ridge
Cefn-y-coed	ridge of the wood
Cefn-y-grug	ridge of heather

Summer and Winter Homes

WALES' EXPOSED UPLANDS *and sheltered valleys mean Welsh farmers long ago developed a form of pastoral farming called* Hafod a Hendre. *Sheep (and formerly cattle) were grazed on the hills in summer, returning to the lower valley- and coastal-pastures over winter. During the colder months the farmer and his family lived in the* hendre, *'old farm' or home farm; but from spring until early autumn, they moved up to the* hafod, *or 'summer house' (from* haf *meaning 'summer ' and* bod *meaning 'dwelling'). This guaranteed fresh grass and year round grazing for the animals, while allowing crops to be grown in the vacated valley fields in summer.*

Ruined hafod in the Rhinog mountains, above Harlech, Gwynedd

Cemaes	bends in the river
Cilmeri	retreat of brambles
Cnwclas	(Knucklas) green hillock
Comins Coch	red commons
Corris	little one
Crai	fresh flowing river
Craig Goch	red rock
Crucadarn	strong cairn
Crucywel	(Crickhowell) Hwyel's mound (personal name)
Crugion	cairns
Crug Mawr	big cairn
Cwmbelan	valley of the round hill
Cwm-bach	little valley
Cwmbach Llechrhyd	little valley of the flat stone ford
Cwm-du	dark valley
Cwmgiedd	valley of the river Giedd
Cwmllinau	valley of the lakes
Darowen	Owain's oaks
Defynnog	land belonging to Deyfwn (personal name)
Derwen-las	green oak tree
Deuthur	two waters (from *deu dwr*)
Dolanog	small stream with water meadows
Dolfach	little meadow
Dolfor	big meadow
Dolforwyn	maiden's meadow
Drum-ddu	black ridge
Drysgol	rough land
Dylife	torrents
Elan	village of the river Elan
Esgairgeiliog	ridge of the cockerel
Fachwen	pale nook or recess
Fan Fawr	big peak
Fan Gihirych	peak near the Gihirych stream
Fan Llia	peak of the Llia stream
Fan Nedd	peak of the river Nedd
Fforest Fawr	big forest
Foel	bald hill
Fron	rounded hillside
Garn Caws	cheese rock (?)
Garth	ridge
Garthmyl	ridge near a mill
Geuffordd	road in a dip

Glasgwm	green valley
Glyntawe	valley of the river Tawe
Grwyne Fechan	little [tributary] of the big river by the wet places
Gwaen Nant-Ddu	mountain pasture of the black stream
Gwaun Ceste Hill	hill pasture or moor of the river Ceste
Gwaun Rhudd	red mountain pasture
Gwenddwr	place near the river Gwenddwr [fair river]
Gwryd	span of two arms
Hengoed	old or former wood
Heniarth	old or former enclosure
Hirnant	long stream valley
Llan	church/enclosure
Llanandras	(Presteigne) St Andreas' church
Llanbadarn Fynydd	St Padarn's church on the mountain
Llanbedr	church of St Peter
Llanbedr Hill	church of St Peter's hill
Llanbister	church of Pister (personal name)
Llanbryn-Mair	church at the hill of St Mary

Huts, Houses and Halls

HOME IS WHERE THE HEART IS, *whatever the language. Over the centuries, Welsh homes have ranged from humble huts and shelters to mason-built mansions. The Welsh for home is* cartref; *while* aelwydydd *(or 'hearth') also refers to home.* Bod *means a home or dwelling, as in Bodfari ('home of Fari').* Bwth *is a hut or cabin; a simple croft, cottage or smallholding is* tyn *or* tyddyn—*a diminutive version of the more common* tŷ, *meaning a house.* Neuadd *means a hall, as in Llwynyneuadd ('grove hall'), and* maenor *a manor.* Cwrt *is a grange or mansion; and* plas—*as in Plas Newydd on Anglesey—means a grand hall or mansion. Finally,* llys *is the Welsh for a court or palace, as in Llysfaen ('stone court'), in Conwy.*

Llandefaelog Tre'r-Graig	church of St Maelog by the settlement on the rock
Llandeglau	church of St Tegle
Llandeilo Graban	church of St Teilo by the corn marigolds
Llandew	church of St David
Llandewi Ystradenni	church of St David in the vale of Nynnid
Llandinam	church of the small fort enclosure
Llandrindod	church of the holy trinity
Llandrinio	church of Trinio (personal name)
Llandulas	church by the river Dulas
Llandysul	church of Tysilio (personal name)
Llaneglwys	enclosure of the church
Llanelwedd	church of Elwedd (personal name)
Llanerfyl	church of St Eurfyl
Llanfair Caereinion	St Mary's church in Caereinion
Llanfair-ym-Muallt	(Builth Wells) St Mary's church in the cow pasture
Llanfechain	church on the plain of the river Cain
Llanfihangel Nant Bran	St Michael's'church on the river Bran (crow)
Llanfihangel Tal-y-llyn	St Michael's church at the end of the lake
Llanfilo	church of Milo (personal name)
Llanfihangel Rhydithon	St Michael's church by the ford on the river Ithon
Llanfihangel-yng-Ngwynfa	St Michael's church on the fair plain
Llanfrynach	church of St Brynach
Llanfyllin	church of St Myllin
Llangadfan	church of Cadfan (personal name)
Llangamarch	church of the river Camarch (horse)
Llangadog	church of St Cadog
Llangedwy	church of Cedwyn (personal name)
Llangoed	church at the wood
Llangors	church at the marsh
Llangunllo	church of St Cynllo
Llangurig	church of St Curig
Llangynidr	church of Cynidr
Llangynog	church of St Cynog
Llanhamlach	church of Anlach (personal name)
Llanidloes	church of St Idloes
Llanigon	church of St Eygon
Llanllugan	church of Llugan (personal name)
Llanrhaeadr-ym-Mochnant	church of the waterfall in Mochnant
Llansantffraid	church of St Bridget/St Ffraid
Llansantffraid-yn-Elfael	church of St Bridget/St Ffraid in Elfael
Llansantffraid-ym-Mechain	church of St Bridget/St Ffraid in Mechain
Llanspyddid	church of St Ysbyddyd
Llansteffan	church of St Ystyffan

Llanwddyn	church of St Gwyddyn
Llanwnnog	church of Gwynnog (personal name)
Llanwrthwl	church of Gwthwl (personal name)
Llanwrtud	church of Gwrtud (personal name)
Llanwyddelan	church of Gwyddelan (personal name)
Llanymynech	church of the monks
Llanllŷr	possibly church of Llyr
Llan-y-wern	church among the alders
Llawr-y-glyn	floor of the glen
Llowes	saint's name (Llywes)
Llwydiarth	grey headland
Llyn Clywedog	lake of the river Clywedog (noisy)
Llyn Efyrnwy	Lake Vyrnwy
Llyswen	white or blessed court
Llywel	[church of] St Llywel
Machynlleth	plain of Cynllaith (personal name)
Maesyfed	(New Radnor) Hyfaidd's field (personal name)
Manafon	plain of Anafon (personal name)

Sheep and Shepherds

SHEEP HAVE BEEN AN ESSENTIAL *part of Wales for centuries. The Welsh word for sheep,* dafad, *occurs in place names such as Defaity (or 'sheep house'), in Anglesey, and Carreg y Ddafad ('sheep rock'), in Gwynedd. A shepherd is* bugail — *as found in Bugeildy or Beguildy ('shepherd's house') in Powys, and Begeli or Begelly ('shepherd's domain'), in Pembrokeshire. Similarly,* lluest *(a 'shepherd's summer shelter'),* corlan *(a 'pinfold') and* lloc *(a sheep 'fold') are reminders of the historic importance of sheep, echoed by the modern place names, Lluest Colliery, Bridgend; Corlannau, Neath Port Talbot; and Lloc, in Flintshire.*

Prize ram at the Tudweiliog show, Llŷn, Gwynedd

Meifod	May house [like *hafod*, 'the summer house']
Merthyr Cynog	burial place of St Cynog
Mochdre	settlement of pigs
Moelfre	bare hill
Mynydd Bwlch-y-Groes	mountain of the pass of the cross
Mynydd Epynt	mountain crossed by a horse track
Mynydd Llangynidr	mountain
Nant Bran	stream valley of the crow
Nant-mel	stream valley of Mael (personal name)
Pant-glas	green or verdant hollow
Pant-y-dwr	hollow of the water
Pen Carreg Dan	flint summit
Penallt mawr	top of the big wooded slope
Pen-celli	top of the hazel grove
Pen-craig	top of the rock
Penegoes	head of the mountain spur
Pen-Maen-Wern	head of the rock of the marsh
Pennant	top of the stream valley
Penystrywaid	trap end
Pentre-bach	little village
Pentre-celyn	village of the river of holly trees
Pen-y-bont	end of the bridge
Pen-y-bont-fawr	end of the big bridge
Pen-y-Fan	top of the peak
Pen-y-Gadair fawr	top of the big chair
Pen-y-Garnedd	top of the cairns
Pen-y-Gwely	top of the resting place or family land
Pistyll Rhaeadr	spring of the waterfall
Pontdolgoch	bridge by the red meadow
Pont Faen	stone bridge
Pont Nedd Fechan	bridge over the little Nedd river
Rhaeadr	waterfall
Rhos-goch	red moor
Sarn	paved way
Sarnau	paved ways
Scethrog	rugged settlement
Sgwd-yr-eira	waterfall of the snow
Sychyn	marsh farm
Talerddig	end of the little hill
Talgarth	end of the enclosure
Tir Rhiwiog	hilly land
Tirabad	land of the abbot

Tor-y-Foel	cleft of the bare hill
Trap	step or rise in the ground
Trefecca	Becca's settlement
Trefeglwys	settlement of the church
Trefyclo	(Knighton) farm by the dyke (Offa's Dyke)
Tregoed	settlement in the wood
Tycrwyn	house of hides or skins
Waun Fach	little meadow
Y Drenewydd	(Newtown) new town
Y Gelli	(Hay on Wye) enclosed forest
Y Trallwng	(Welshpool) marshy or muddy area
Yr Allt	the wooded hillside
Yscir Fawr	big ridge
Yscir Fechan	little ridge
Ystrad Fellte	vale of the river Mellte
Ystradgynlais	vale of Cynlais

Cattle and Pigs

FARM ANIMALS HAVE ALWAYS ENLIVENED *the Welsh countryside. The Welsh word for a cow is* buwch *or* gwartheg, *while* mochyn *means 'pig'. Places named after them include Nant y Fuwch ('cow valley'), in Powys, and Mochdre ('pig farmstead'), with examples in both Denbighshire and Powys. Related words include cow house or beudy, as in Beudy-mawr ('big cow house'), in Gwynedd; milk or llaeth, as in Llaethdy ('milk house'), in Powys; and butter or menyn, as in Brynmenyn ('hill of butter'), in the Vale of Glamorgan. Further pig-related names include Castell Moch ('stronghold of pigs'), in Powys, and Nant-y-banw ('valley of piglets'), in Monmouthshire.*

Pembrokeshire/Penfro

Abercych	confluence of the rives Cuch and Teifi
Abergwaun	(Fishguard) mouth of the river Gwaun
Abereiddi	mouth of the river Eiddi
Afon Teifi	dark or flowing river
Berea	Berea chapel (biblical name)
Blaen-ffos	top of the ditch
Bryn Henllan	hill of the old church
Brynberian	hill of Berian (personal name)
Bwlch-y-Groes	pass of the cross
Bwncath	buzzard (old inn name)
Caer Farchell	St Marchell's stronghold
Carregwastad	flat rock
Carew	fort of many ditches
Castell Hendre	castle of the old settlement
Coedcanlas	Canlas's wood (personal name)
Cilgerran	nook of Cerran (personal name)
Cleddau	sword river
Clunderwen	meadow of the oak tree
Crinow	dry, parched lands
Croes-goch	red cross
Crymych	crooked stream
Dinas	fort or citadel
Eglwyswrw	church of Erow (personal name)
Felindre Farchog	farm around the knight's mill
Foel Dyrch	bare hill of the boar
Hermon	Hermon chapel (biblical name)
Llanbedr Felffre	church of St Peter in Efelffre
Llandewi Felffre	church of St David in Efelffre
Llantysilio	church of St Tysilio
Llandre Isaf	lower church village
Llangloffan	church of Cloffan (personal name)
Llangolman	church of St Colman
Llanrhian	church of St Rhian
Llanteg	fair or lovely stream
Llanwnda	church of St Gwndaf
Llawhaden	church of Huadain (personal name)
Llys-y-fran	court of the raven [ie: ruined court]
Maenclochog	rocks sounding like a bell
Manorowen	estate of Gnawan (personal name)
Mathry	place of grief
Mynachlog-ddu	black monastery

Mynydd Caregog	stony mountain
Mynydd Melyn	yellow mountain
Mynydd Preseli	mountain of Preseli [thicket]
Penfro	(Pembroke) end of the land
Pen-ffordd	end of the road
Pen-rhiw	end of the hillside
Pentre Ifan	village of Ifan (personal name)
Pen-y-Bryn	top of the hill
Pen-y-Cwm	head of the valley
Pontfaen	stone bridge
Porthgain	fair bay
Rhosili	Sulien's moor headland
Solfach	(Solva) poor land
Tegryn	fair hill
Tre-cŵn	settlement of dogs
Tregarne	settlement of the cairn
Trwyn-y-bwa	the bowed promontory
Ynys Daullyn	island of two pools

Holy Wells

SPRINGS AND WELLS *have been held sacred since time out of mind. To the ancient Celts they were the home of gods and goddesses. But from the 7th century onwards these pagan wells were cleverly adopted and 'purified' by the Christian church. Over 200 early churches across Wales are built near holy wells. The most famous example is St Winifred's Well at Holywell, in Flintshire. Nonetheless, Wales' holy wells were used for centuries to ensure good luck, restore health, and invoke blessings and curses; and many are still visited for the same reasons today.*

Carmarthenshire/Caerfyrddin

Aberarad	mouth of the river Arad
Abergiar	confluence of the chicken-like stream
Abergorlech	mouth of the river Gorlech (gritty)
Abergwili	mouth of the river Gwili (kind, generous?)
Aber-nant	confluence of streams
Afon Annell	silver river
Afon Bran	crow or dark river
Afon Cothi	scouring river
Afon Crychan	rippling river
Afon Cynin	St Cynin's river
Afon Cywyn	plagued river
Afon Gwendraeth	river Gwendraeth (of the white shore)
Afon Gwenlais	white river
Afon Gwili	river of Gwili (personal name)
Afon Morlais	great river
Afon Taf	dark or flowing river
Afon Tywi	dark or flowing river
Alltwalis	wooded slope by the walls
Bancffosfelen	hill of the yellow ditch
Bancycapel	bank of the chapel
Bancyfelin	bank of the mill
Bethlehem	Bethlehem chapel (biblical name)
Blaenwaun	head of the moorland pasture
Blaen-y-coed	head of the wood
Brechfa	speckled place
Bronwydd	rounded hillside of trees
Brynaman	hill near the river Aman
Brynbeddau	hillside of graves
Brynmyrddin	Myrddin's hill (personal name)
Brynteifi	hill on the river Teifi
Bwlchnewydd	new pass
Bynea	bitterns
Caeo	land of Caeo (personal name)
Caerfyrddin	(Carmarthen) fortress on the sea
Capel Cefnberach	chapel on the sharp ridge
Capel Dewi	chapel of St David
Capel Hendre	chapel near the winter farm
Capel Isaac	Isaac's chapel
Capel Iwan	Iwan's'chapel (personal name)
Capel Llanlluan	St Lluan's chapel
Carmarthen Van	Carmarthen peak, from 'Caerfyrddin'

Carmel	Carmel (biblical name)
Carn Fadog	Madog's cairn (personal name)
Carreg Cennen	[castle on a] rock beside the river Cennen
Carreg-lwyd	grey rock
Castell Meurig	Meurig's castle (personal name)
Castell-moel	bare castle
Castellnewydd Emlyn	(Newcastle Emlyn) new castle in Emlyn
Castell Pigyn	castle on the peak
Castellrhingyll	steward's castle
Cefn-coed	wooded ridge
Cefneithin	gorse covered ridge
Cofnsidan	cotton grass ridge
Cefn-y-pant	ridge of the mill
Cilsant	nook or retreat of the saint
Cil-y-cwm	shelter or retreat in the valley
Cil-maen-llwyd	shelter of grey stone
Cloigyn	bundle of straw
Craig Derllwyn	rock by the oak grove
Croes-y-ceiliog	cross of the cockerel

Hermits and Holymen

EARLY CHRISTIAN MISSIONARIES IN WALES *during the sixth and seventh centuries often led solitary lives. They lived in simple cells within a small enclosure, or* llan, *perhaps gathering disciples as their reputation spread. The Welsh for hermit is* meudwy, *as in Ynys Meudwy (or 'hermit's island'), in Glamorgan, or Rhyd-y-Meudwy ('hermit's ford'), in Denbighshire. A hermit's retreat or refuge is* cil, *as in Cilgerran, in Pembrokeshire. More unexpectedly, Dyserth in Denbighshire takes its name from the Latin* desertum, *which also means a hermit's retreat.*

Carved head, Beguildy, Powys

Crugiau Rhos-wen	cairns on the white moor
Crug Siarl	cairn of Charles
Crug-y-bar	cairn by the sandbank
Crwbin	outcrop or hillock
Cryngae	withered hedge
Cwmbach	little valley
Cwm Cynnen	disputed valley
Cwmfelin Boeth	valley of the burnt mill
Cwmfelinmynach	valley of the monastery's mill
Cwmffrwd	valley of the spring
Cwmgwili	valley of the river Gwili
Cwm-mawr	big valley
Cwm-pen-craig	valley of the head of the rock
Cwm-y-glo	valley of coal
Cwmduad	valley of the river Duad
Cwrt Bryn-y-beirdd	court on the bards' hill
Cydweli	(Kidwelly) land of Cadwel
Cynghordy	kennel or gate house
Cynwyl Elfed	[church of] Cynwyl in Elfed
Dafen	spring where sheep graze
Derllys	great court
Dolaucothi	water meadows of the river Cothi
Dre-fach	little settlement
Drysgol	rough mountain
Efailwen	white smithy
Eglwys Gymyn	church of the endowment
Felindre	settlement of the mill
Felinfoel	mill hill
Felin-gwm-isaf	mill of the lower valley
Felin-gwm-uchaf	mill of the upper valley
Felin-wen	white mill
Ffairfach	little fairground
Ffynnon-ddrain	briar well
Garnbica	pointed cairn
Garnant	the rough stream
Gelliwen	white or fair grove
Glanaman	bank of the river Aman
Glynteg	lovely glen
Gogofau	caves
Gorslas	green marsh
Gwernogle	marshy place
Gwyddgrug	prominent burial mound or cairn
Horeb	Horeb chapel (biblical name)

Lacharn	(Laugharne) bright rock
Llanarthne	church of the headland or enclosure
Llanboidy	stream of the cowshed (from nant beudy)
Llanbydderi	church of the deaf [to the calling of Christ]
Llanddarrog	church of Darrog (personal name)
Llanddwror	church of the water drinkers (teetotallers)
Llandeilo	church of St Teilo
Llanymddyfri	(Llandovery) church near the waters
Llandybie	church of Tybiau (personal name)
Llandyfaelog	church of Tyfaelog (personal name)
Llanegwad	church of St Egwad
Llanelli	church of Elli (personal name)
Llanfallteg	church of Ballteg (personal name)
Llanfihangel-ar-arth	St Michael's church of Iorath (personal name)
Llanfynydd	church on a mountain
Llangadog	church of St Cadog
Llangain	church of Cain(personal name)
Llangathen	church of Cathen (personal name)

Early Churches

AT THE LAST COUNT, *there were 608 places in Wales beginning with the commonest of all Welsh place name elements:* llan. *Originally it meant a clearing or enclosure; and this sense is retained in words for various types of yard such as* perllan *('orchard'),* ydlan *('granary'), and* gwinllan *('vineyard'). But when Christian missionaries set up enclosed cells across the country in the sixth and seventh centuries, the word came to mean a church, and later a parish church. In many cases,* llan *is associated with either a word describing the church's location, as in* Llanrhaeadr *('church of the waterfall') or* Llanfynydd *('church of the mountain'), or with a patron saint as, for example, in* Llanberis *('church of St Peris') or* Llanbedr *('church of St Peter').*

Llangyndeyrn	church of St Cyndeyrn
Llangennech	church of St Cennyd
Llanglydwen	church of Clydwyn (personal name)
Llangunnor	church of Cynfor (personal name)
Llangynin	church of Cynin (personal name)
Llangynog	church of Cynog (personal name)
Llanllwch	church by boggy ground
Llanllwni	church of Lleweni (personal name)
Llannon	church of St Non
Llanpumsaint	church of five saints
Llansadurnen	church of St Sadyrnin
Llansadwrn	church of St Sadwrn
Llansaint	church of the saints
Llansteffan	church of St Stephen
Llanwinio	church of Gwynio (personal name)
Llanwrda	church of St Gwrdaf
Llanybydder	church of the once deaf (to God's word)
Llwynhendy	grove by the old house
Login	little polluted river
Meinciau	benches or hillocks
Maesybont	field by the bridge
Meidrim	middle ridge
Myddfai	meadow of the round hollow
Mynydd Cynros	mountain of the chisel-shaped promontory
Mynydd Figyn	mountain of the marsh
Mynydd Llanllwni	mountain of the church of Llewenni
Mynydd Llanybydder	Llanbydder mountain
Mynydd Mallaen	mountain of Mallaen
Mynydd Pencarreg	mountain of the head of the rock
Mynydd Sylen	St Sulien's mount
Nantgaredig	kind or gentle stream
Pantyffynnon	well hollow
Pencader	head of the seat or stronghold
Pentywyn	(Pendine) top of the sand dunes
Pentre Gwenlais	village near the white stream
Pentre-cwrt	village of the court
Penybanc	top of the bank
Penygroes Saron	top of the Saron chapel crossroads
Pontantwn	Anthony's bridge
Pont-ar-gothi	bridge over the river Cothi
Pontarsais	Englishman's bridge
Pont-tyweli	(Pontwelly) bridge on the river Tyweli

Pontyates	Yates' bridge (personal name)
Pontyberem	bridge at the mouth of the river Beran
Pumpsaint	five saints
Pwll Trap	trap pool [mill dam or fish trap]
Rhandirmwyn	land of minerals
Rhos	moorland
Rhydaman	(Ammanford) ford on the river Aman
Rhydargaeau	ford near the fields
Rhydcymerau	ford where the rivers meet
Talley	from talyllchau, end of the waters
Talog	dirty [ford]
Trelech	settlement of the flat rocks
Trimsaran	ridge of Saeran (personal name)
Twynllanan	mound by the church
Tycroes	house of the cross
Waunclunda	good meadow common

Places of Worship

AFTER LLAN, *which now means a parish church, the next most common religious Welsh place name elements are eglwys, capel and betws. Eglwys also means church and comes from the Latin* ecclesia. *As you'd expect,* capel *means chapel; either a 'chapel of ease' built for people who lived too far from the main parish church or, more often, a later nonconformist chapel or meeting house. The meaning of betws is more complex. It's usually said to derive from the Old English* bed hus, *or 'bead house', meaning a prayer house or oratory. But in parts of North Wales betws clearly refers to a wooded slope of birch trees—from the Latin* betula *and the Old Welsh* betguos.

Swansea/Abertawe

Abertawe	(Swansea) mouth of the river Tawe
Blaen-y-maes	head of the field
Bolgoed	wooded hillock
Bon-y-maen	place at the bottom of the stone
Brynhyfryd	happy hill
Bwlchymynydd	mountain pass
Cae-mawr	big field
Carn-glas	green cairn
Cefn Drum	ridge of the mountain crest
Clydach	[river] running over flat rocks
Craig-cefn-parc	rock on pasture ridge
Craig Fawr	big rock
Cwm-du	dark valley
Cwm Gwyn	blessed valley
Dynfant	deep valley
Faerdre	steward's farm, demesne
Felindre	settlement of the mill
Fforest Fach	little forest
Garn-swllt	shilling or treasure cairn
Gendros	ridge on the moor
Glais	the stream
Gorseinon	bog of Einion (personal name)
Graig Trewyddfa	rock of the settlement by the memorial cairn
Gwernfadog	alder marsh of Madog (personal name)
Hafod	summer dwelling
Hendrefoilan	winter dwelling on the little hill
Hendy	the old house
Heol-las	green road
Llandewi	church of St David
Llanmadog	church of Madog (personal name)
Llanrhidian	church of Rhidian (personal name)
Llansamlet	church of Samled (personal name)
Pantlasau	hollow of streams
Pen-clawdd	end of the ditch
Pengelli	end of the briar patch
Penlle'r-gaer	top of the fortified place
Pennardd	top of the headland
Pen-maen	head of the stone
Pen Pyrod	(Worm's Head) snake's head
Pen-Rhys	(Penrice) hill of Rhys (personal name)

Pentre-bach	little village
Pentre-chwyth	windy village
Pentre-dŵr	village by the water
Pentre-poeth	burnt settlement
Pen-y-lan	top of the mound
Penyrheol	end of the road
Pontarddulais	bridge over the river Dulais (dark stream)
Pontlliw	bridge over the gleaming river
Porth Einon	port of Einion (personal name)
Rhosili	Sulien's headland
Rhydypandy	ford of the fulling mill
Tircanol	middle land
Trebannws	settlement in the cotton grass
Treboeth	burnt or parched settlement
Treforys	(Morriston) Morris's town
Tre-gwyr	(Gowerton) settlement in the curved land
Waunarlwydd	lord's moor
Ynystawe	island of the river Tawe

Monks and Monasteries

MONKS, MONASTERIES AND MARTYRS *often feature in Welsh place names. The Welsh for monk is* mynach*, as in Llanymynech ('church of the monks'), in Powys, while* mynechdid *means monastery, as in Efenechdyd ('the monastery' or 'monastic grange'), in Denbighshire. A monk's cell is* cell*, as in Cellan (or 'small cell') near Lampeter, in Ceredigion; while the Welsh for a monastic cloister is* clas*. Finally,* merthyr *is Welsh for a martyr—so that, for example, Merthyr Tydfil, in South Wales, means the place where Saint Tydfil was either killed or buried.*

Neath, Port Talbot/ Castell-nedd, Port Talbot

Aberdulais	where the rivers Dulais and Nedd meet
Abergregan	mouth of the river Cregan (shells)
Abergregan Dyffryn	vale of the mouth of the river Cregan
Abergwynfi	mouth of the river Gwynfi
Afon Dulais	river Dulais
Afon Egel	sowbread plant river
Afon Nedd	(Neath) river Nedd
Alltwen	white hillside
Baglan	[place of] Baglan's church (personal name)
Blaengwrach	source of the river Gwrach (witch/hag)
Blaengwynfi	source of the river Gwynfi
Bryn	hill
Bryn-coch	red hill
Castell Nedd	(Neath) castle on the river Nedd
Cefn Mawr	big ridge
Cilybebyll	shelter or grove of the tents
Cilffriw	sheltered by the prominent rock
Cilmaen-gwyn	nook or recess of the white stone
Cimla	common
Craig Llangiwg	rock church of Ciwg (personal name)
Craig-y-llyn	rock of the lake
Croeserw	cross acre
Crynant	place near the river Creunant
Cwmafan	valley of the river Afan
Cwmllynfell	valley of the river Llynfell
Cymer	confluence of the river Afan
Dyffryn	valley
Dyffryn Cellwen	valley of the white cell
Efail-fach	little smithy
Farteg	most beautiful place
Foel Mynyddau	bare hill of the mountains
Gellinudd	Nudd's grove (legendary name)
Glyncorrwg	valley of the river Corrwg
Glyn-neath	valley of the river Nedd
Godre'r-graig	bottom of the cliff
Gwaun Cae Gurwen	marshy hemlock field
Hir Fynydd	long mountain

Margam	Morgan (personal name)
Moel-ton-mawr	bare hill of large meadow lands
Moel-yr-Hydd	bare hill of the stag
Mynydd Marchywel	Hywels' steed's mountain
Mynydd Margam	Morgan's mountain
Mynydd-allt-y-grug	mountain of the hillside of heather
Pen Rhiwfawr	top of the long slope
Penller Fedwen	end of the site of white birches
Pontardawe	bridge on the river Tawe
Pont-rhyd-y-fen	bridge by the ford on the river Afan
Pwll-y-glaw	rain pool
Resolfen	stubble upland; gazing place
Rhos	moorland
Rhyd-y-fro	ford in the vale
Taibach	little houses
Tonna	meadow lands, grassy plots
Ystalyfera	hay stall

Viking Place Names

VIKING RAIDERS SAILING AROUND WALES *during the ninth to eleventh centuries gave Nordic names to sandbanks, skerries, islands, headlands and other coastal features useful as navigational markers. The Norse word for a large island, for example, was ey; a smaller islet was holmr; an isolated rock in the sea, or skerry, was sker; a bay was vik; and a sandbank eyrr. Viking place names around the Welsh coast include: Swansea ('Sveinn's island' or 'sea island') and Ramsey ('Hrafn's island'); Grassholm ('grass island); Emsger (Em's skerry); Musselwick ('mussel bay'); and Point of Ayr, in North Wales, which contains the Norse word for a 'sandbank'.*

The Skerries, off Carmel Head, Isle of Anglesey

Bridgend/Pen-y-bont ar Ogwr

Afon Ewenni	river Ewenny
Abercynffig	(Aberkenfig) mouth of the river Cynffig
Afon Garw	river Garw (rough)
Afon Llynfi	river Llynfi
Abergarw	confluence of the rivers Garw and Ogwr
Betws	prayer house
Blaengarw	source of the river Garw
Brechfa	speckled hillside
Brynmenyn	butter hill (rich cattle grazing)
Bryngarw	craggy hill
Brynna	hills
Cefn Cribwr	back of the ridge
Coety	house in the wood
Cwmfelin	shallow mill valley
Cynffig	(Kenfig) [place on the] river Cynffig
Gilfach Goch	the red nook
Glanllynfi	lake shore
Goetre-hen	(Coytrahen) old settlement by the wood
Heol-y-Cyw	the young animal's road
Llangeinor	church of St Cain the virgin
Maesteg	fair field
Merthyr Mawr	burial place of St Myfor
Mynedd Caerau	mountain of forts
Mynedd Llangeinwyr	mountain of the church of St Ceinwyr
Nant-y-moel	valley of the bare hill
Pencoed	end of the wood
Pen-y-bont ar Ogwr	(Bridgend) end of the bridge over the river Ogwr
Pontycymer	bridge over the confluence
Pont-yr-hyl	hill bridge
Porthcawl	sea kale bay
Tondu	black unploughed grassland
Y Sger	sheer rock

"Wales, where the past still lives. Where every place has its tradition, every name its poetry, and where the people still know this past, this tradition, this poetry, and live with it ..."

Matthew Arnold, *On the Study of Celtic Literature*, 1866

Mines and Quarries

GOLD, SILVER, LEAD, COPPER, SLATE, LIMESTONE AND COAL *have all been mined or quarried in Wales for centuries. There are even copper mines on the Great Orme, in North Wales, first worked in the Bronze Age. The Welsh word* mwyn *means both 'mineral ore' and 'mine';* cwar *or* chwarel *means 'quarry'; while* glo *is Welsh for 'coal'. Examples of places containing these elements include: Mwynglawdd or Minera ('mine'), in Wrexham, and both Pant-y-mwyn ('the mine hollow') and Rhyd-y-mwyn ('the ore ford') in the old lead mining area of Flintshire. Chwarel y Fan ('quarry on a high hill') in the Black Mountains, and Cwm-y-glo ('valley of coal'), near Caernarfon, also reflect man's age-old exploitation of the earth.*

Rhondda Cynon Taf

Aberaman	mouth of the river Aman (personal name)
Abercynon	mouth of the river Cynon (personal name)
Aberdâr	mouth of the river Dar (oak trees)
Aber-nant	mouth of the stream
Beddau	graves
Blaen-y-cwm	end of the valley
Bodringallt	steward's dwelling
Brynna	hills
Brynsadler	hill of the saddler
Bwlch-y-clawdd	gap in the bank
Cae Maen	standing stone field
Cefn-pennar	ridge at the end of the arable land
Cilfynydd	mountain recess or shelter
Clydach	river name (rocky bed)
Cwmaman	valley of the river Aman
Cwm-bach	little valley
Cwmdar	valley of the river Dar
Cwm-Parc	valley of the parkland
Cymmer	where the rivers meet
Dinas	fortress
Efail-isaf	lower smithy
Ffaldau	pens, pinfolds
Ffynnon Taf	(Taff's Well) well on the river Taff
Groes-faen	the stone cross
Hirwaun	long moor
Llanilid	church of St Ilid
Llantrisant	church of three saints
Llanilltud Faerdref	church of St Illtud at the demesne
Llanharan	church of Aaron (personal name)
Llwydcoed	grey wood
Llwynypia	grove of magpies
Mynydd Merthyr	mountain of the martyr
Mynydd-y-glo	coal mountain
Penderyn	bird's head
Penrhiwceibr	hilltop of the arched branches
Pentre poeth	burnt settlement
Pen-y-coedcae	hill by the hedged field
Pen-y-graig	top of the rock
Pen-y-groes	cross end
Pen Rhys	Rhys's top

Pen-y-waun	end of the meadow
Pont-y-gwaith	works' bridge
Pontypridd	bridge of the mud house
Rhondda	chattering river
Rhydfelen	yellow ford
Tonypandy	fulling mill on a grassy plot
Tonyrefail	smithy on a grassy plot
Trealaw	settlement of Alaw (personal name)
Trecynon	settlement of Cynon (personal name)
Trefforest	forest settlement
Trehafod	settlement of the summer dwelling
Treherbert	Herbert's town
Treorci	settlement on the Gorci stream
Tyn-y-nant	smallholding of the valley
Ynys-boeth	warm or parched river meadow
Ynys-y-bŵl	meadow by the pool (or an inn name)
Ynys-hir	long island
Ystrad	wide valley

Welsh Chapels

THE WELSH CHAPEL, *or* capel, *is an iconic part of Wales. More than 6,000 nonconformist chapels were built across Wales during the religious revivals of the nineteenth and early twentieth centuries. By the First World War almost every town, village and hamlet had its own Baptist, Congregationalist, Methodist, Presbyterian or Unitarian meeting house. The buildings varied from converted barns and crude corrugated iron sheds to elaborate edifices with grand facades in the larger towns and cities. Sadly, today the widespread collapse in chapel-going means many chapels are either now derelict, converted or threatened with demolition; with only the finest listed and protected for posterity.*

Merthyr Tydfil/Merthyr Tudful

Abercannaid	where the Cannaid stream joins the river Taf
Aber-fan	where the Fan stream joins the river Taf
Bedlinog	house near the Llwynog stream
Cefncoedycymmer	wooded ridge at the confluence
Cwmfelin	valley of the mill
Dowlais	black spring
Dyffryn	broad vale
Heolgerrig	stone road
Maerdy	steward's house
Merthyr Tydfil	burial place of St Tudful (personal name)
Pengarn-ddu	top of the black cairn
Pentre-bach	little village
Pontsticill	bridge near the stile
Treharris	Harris' town
Trelewis	Lewis' town
Troed-y-rhiw	foot of the hill
Trwyn-yr-odyn	long hill of the kiln
Twyn Croes	mound of the cross

Caerphilly/Caerffili

Aberbargod	confluence at the border
Abercarn	mouth of the river Carn (cairn)
Abertridwr	confluence of three streams
Abertyswg	confluence of the rivers Tyswyg and Rhymni
Afon Rhymni	river Rhymni (auger or foretell)
Argoed	boundary
Bargod	boundary
Bedwas	grove of birch trees
Bedwellty	house of Mellteu (personal name)
Brithdir	speckled land
Bryn	hill
Caerffili	(Caerphilly) fort of Philip or Ffili
Cefn Hengoed	ridge of the old wood
Croes-wen	white cross
Cwmcarn	valley of the cairn
Cwmfelin-fach	valley of the little mill
Deri	oak trees
Gelli-gaer	grove of the fort
Gelli-groes	grove of the cross
Gilfach	nook or retreat

Hengoed	old or former wood
Llanbradach	bank of the Bradach stream
Llechrhyd	flat stone ford
Machen	plain of Cein (personal name)
Maesycwmer	field where the rivers meet
Mynydd Eglwysilan	mountain of the church of St Sulian
Mynydd Maen	stone mountain
Pengam	crooked head
Penmaen	top of the rock
Pentwyn-mawr	top of the big mound
Pontllan-fraith	bridge by the speckled pool
Pont-y-waun	bridge of the meadow
Risca	tree bark
Senghennydd	Sangan's land (personal name)
Tirphil	Philip's land (personal name)
Ynys-ddu	black island
Ystrad Mynach	vale of the monk

Norman Place Names

FOLLOWING THE NORMAN CONQUEST, *castles were built across Wales to crush any threat of rebellion. They are commonest in Pembrokeshire, the rest of South Wales and along the Welsh Marches. The Norman 'Landsker' colony in south Pembrokeshire featured strongholds at Pembroke, Haverdfordwest, Carew, Manorbier and elsewhere. Many of their Norman French and Flemish place names describe the castles' locations. Beaumaris on Anglesey, for example, takes its name from the French for 'beautiful marsh'. Similarly, the name Mold comes from the French Mont-hault, meaning 'high hill'; while Montgomery in Powys is named after its namesake, Montgommery, in the Calvados region of France.*

Beaumaris Castle, Isle of Anglesey

Blaenau Gwent

Abertyleri	(Abertillery) mouth of the river Teleri
Blaina	uplands
Bryn Bach	little hill
Brynmawr	big hill
Cwmtyleri	valley of the river Tyleri
Glynebwy	(Ebbw Vale) valley of the river Ebwy (wild colt)
Llanhiledd	church of St Heledd
Man-moel	bare place
Mynydd-carn-y-cefn	mountain of the cairn on the ridge
Mynydd Coety	wood house mountain
Nant-y-glo	valley of coal
Tredegar	settlement of Tegyr (personal name)

Torfaen

Abersychan	mouth of the river Sychan (dries up)
Blaenafon	source of the river
Croes-y-ceiliog	cock's cross
Cwmbrân	valley of the river Brân (dark)
Garn Diffaith	wasted cairn
Henllys	old or former court
Llantarnam	stream of Teyrnon
Pont-hir	long bridge
Pontnewydd	new bridge
Pont-y-pŵl	(Pontypool) bridge of ap Hywel (personal name)
Tal-y-waun	moor end

Vale of Glamorgan/Bro Morgannwg

Aberddawan	(Aberthaw) mouth of the river Ddawan
Brynmenyn	hill of butter (rich grazing)
Clawdd-coch	red dyke
Coedrhiglan	Raglan's wood (family name)
Cogan	polder (land reclaimed from the sea)
Col-huw	wood by the shallows
Dinas Powys	fort of the pagans (from the Latin *pagus*)
Ewenni	place near the river Ewenni
Llanbydderi	brook of Bydderi (personal name)
Llanbleddian	church of St Bleddian

Llancadle	church of St Cadle
Llancarfan	valley of Carfan (personal name)
Llandochau	church of St Dochau
Llangan	church of Canna (personal name)
Llan-maes	church in the open countryside
Llantrithyd	stream of Rhirid (personal name)
Llantilltud	church of Illtud (personal name)
Llyswyrny	court of Gwrinydd (personal name)
Maendy	the stone house
Penarth	top of the headland
Pendeulwyn	head of two groves
Penllyn	head of the lake
Pen-marc	horse's head
Pentremeurig	Meurig's homestead (personal name)
Tre-os	goose farm
Trerhyngyll	settlement of the sergeant
Y Bont-faen	(Cowbridge) stone bridge
Ystradowen	Owain's wide valley

A494
Wrexham
Wrecsam
(A541)

MOLD
Historic Market Town
YR WYDDGRUG
ef Farchnad Hanesydd

Cardiff
Caerdydd
(A470)

English Place Names

ENGLAND HAS INFLUENCED WALES *for many centuries. So English place names are often found in Wales, especially in Pembrokeshire in the south, and in Flintshire, Denbighshire and the other Welsh borderlands to the north. Some are Old English or Saxon names—like Wrexham ('Wrytel's water meadow'). Some are anglicized versions of original Welsh names—as in Mold (from 'mount' or 'mound'), itself a variant of Yr Wyddgrug ('the prominent mound'). Others are English mispronunciations of earlier Welsh names, as in Cardiff, derived from Caerdydd ('fort on the river Taf'), or Carmarthen, from Caerfyrddin (or 'fortress on the sea').*

Cardiff/Caerdydd

Afon Elái	river Elái
Afon Taf	river Taff
Caerau	forts
Caerdydd	(Cardiff) fort on the river Taf
Castell Coch	red castle
Cefn Onn	ridge of the ash trees
Creigiau	cliffs
Cyncoed	hound wood
Gabalfa	the ferry place
Llandaf	church on the river Taf
Llanedern	church of St Edern
Llanisien	church of St Isien
Llanrhymni	church by the river Rhymni
Llys-faen	stone court
Pengam	crooked top
Pentre-baen	Payne's settlement on a ridge (personal name)
Pentwyn	head of the dune
Pentyrch	boar hill
Plasnewydd	new hall
Pontprennau	bridge of trees (ie: wooden)
Radur	prayer house
Rhiwbeina	crow's hill
Rhydlafar	chattering ford
Sblott	from the English, 'God's plot'
Tongwynlais	fallow land of the white stream
Tredelerch	(Rumney) Elerch's settlement (personal name)
Trelai	(Ely) settlement on the river Elai
Tremorfa	marsh settlement
Tyllgoed	(Fairwater) dark woods
Waun Treoda	moor by Goda's settlement (personal name)
Y Wenallt	white or blessed wooded slope

"Wales is a singular noun but a plural experience."

Dai Smith, *Wales! Wales?*, 1984

Newport/Casnewydd

Betws	prayer house
Caerleon	fort of the legion
Casnewydd	(Newport) new castle
Cefn	ridge
Eglwys y Drindod	(Christchurch) church of the Trinity
Llanbedr	church of St Peter
Llandyfawg	church of St Tyfawg
Llandyfenni	church of the honoured lady
Llanwern	church at the alder grove
Parc Seymour	Seymour's parkland
Pen-hw	place at the ridge
Penrhos	top of the high moor
Rhiwderyn	slope of thc bird
Trefonnen	(Nash) settlement by the ash tree

Funny Place Names

To the superficial English ear, some Welsh place names seem amusing. Without understanding their true meanings, they can sound either silly or obscene. Favourites include: Sblot (from the English 'God's plot'), in Cardiff; Plwmp (meaning 'water pump'), in Ceredigion; and Rhiwbeina (or 'crow's hill'), also in Cardiff. Better still are: Shwt (possibly from the English [coal] 'chute'), in Bridgend; Pantygog (or 'cuckoo hollow'), in Monmouthshire; and Penisa'r-waun ('bottom end of the field'), in Gwynedd. Strangest of all, however, is probably Sodom (named after a nonconformist chapel) near Bodfari, in Denbighshire, North Wales.

Road sign to Sodom, Denbighshire

Monmouthshire/Mynwy

Abergavenny	(see Y Fenni)
Afon Honddu	quiet river
Afon Mynwy	river Mynwy
Afon Troddi	rushing river
Afon Wysg	(River Usk) river abounding in fish
Bedwellte	home of Mellteu (personal name)
Betws Newydd	new prayer house
Brynbuga	(Usk) Buga's hill (personal name)
Bryngwyn	white hill
Casgwent	(Chepstow) fort of Gwent
Clydach	fast, stony river
Coed-y-paun	wood of the peacock
Gaerllwyd	grey or pale fort
Gilwern	nook near the marsh of alders
Glascoed	green wood
Goetre	home in the wood
Gofilon	tongs or pincers
Gwehelog	mixed or motley
Gwernesni	marsh of Esni (personal name)
Llandeilo Gresynni	church of Teilo (personal name) at Cresynych
Llanarth	church at the ridge
Llanbadog	church of St Padog
Llanddewi Rhydderch	church of St David
Llanddewi-nant-hodni	(Llanthony) church of Dewi in the vale of the Honddu
Llandegfedd	church of Tegfedd (personal name)
Llandenni	church of St Tenni
Llanelen	church of Elen (personal name)
Llanfair Iscoed	church of Mary below the wood
Llan-ffwyst	church of St Ffwyst
Llanfrechfa	church at Brechfa (speckled field)
Llangadog	church of St Cadog of the wooded lake
Llangwm	church of the valley
Llangwm Isaf	church of the lower valley
Llangybi	church of St Cybi
Llanhenwg	church of Henog (personal name)
Llanishen	church of St Isien
Llanllywel	church of Llywel (personal name)
Llanofer	church of St Myfor
Llan-soe	church of St Tysoe
Llantrisant	church of three saints
Llanfable	church of Mable (personal name)

Llanfetherin	church of St Gwytherin
Llanfihangel Crucornau	church of archangel Michael at Crugornau
Maerdy	the steward's house
Mynydd Bach	little mountain
Nant-y-banw	valley of piglets
Pandy	fulling mill
Penallt	top of the slope
Penperllenni	hill of the orchards
Penrhos	end of the moor headland
Pen-twyn	top of the hillock
Pwllmeurig	pit near the river Meurig
Tal-y-coed	front of the wood
Tredynog	ferny farm
Trefynwy	(Monmouth) town on the river Mynwy
Tregare	settlement near the fort
Tryleg	farm by the flat rock
Y Fenni	(Abergavenny) the place by the ironworks
Ysgyryd Fawr	big rough

Naming America?

HOW DID AMERICA GET ITS NAME? *Most people agree the New World was named after an early explorer, the Italian merchant and map maker Amerigo Vespucci, whose ships sailed up the east coast of America around 1500. However, enthusiasts insist there is an earlier claimant. Controversial evidence suggests America was actually named after a Welshman, Richard Amerike, who is known to have funded several of the famous explorer John Cabot's earlier voyages of discovery in the late 1400s. The surname Amerike probably derives from ap Meuric—the Welsh for 'son of Maurice'. But was he really the true founder of America?*

Old cigarette card showing Amerigo Vespucci

GRANDES FIGURES HISTORIQUES DE L'AMERIQUE LATINE
1. - AMERIC VESPUCE (1451-1512).
Vespuce tente le passage d'un océan dans l'autre.
PRODUITS LIEBIG: améliorent la cuisine.

Further Reading

Books

Anon., *Welsh Place Names*, John Jones Publishing, 1996

Davies, Brian, *Welsh Place-names Unzipped*, Y Lolfa, Ceredigion, 2003

Davies, Dewi, *Welsh Place-names and their meanings*, Brecon and Radnor Express, no date

Davies, Elwyn (editor), *A Gazeteer of Welsh Place Names*, University of Wales Press, 1996

Leaver, Tony, *Pronouncing Welsh Place-names*, Gwasg Carreg Gwalch, Llanrwst, 1998

Lewis, D Geraint, *A Check-List of Welsh Place-names*, Gomer, Ceredigion, 2007

Lias, Anthony, *A Guide to Welsh Place-Names*, Gwasg Carreg Gwalch, Llanrwst, 1994

Ordnance Survey, *A Glossary of the Most Common Welsh Elements used on Maps of Wales*, Southampton, 2004

Owen, Hywel Wyn, & Morgan, Richard, *Dictionary of the Place-names of Wales*, Gomer, Ceredigion, 2007

Websites

BBC Wales:	www.bbc.co.uk/wales/whatsinaname/
Ordnance Survey:	www.ordnancesurvey.co.uk/oswebsite/freefun/didyouknow/
	placenames/docs/welsh_guide.pdf
University of Wales:	www.e-gymraeg.co.uk/enwaulleoedd/amr/
	www.e-gymraeg.co.uk/enwaucymru/
Welsh Place names:	www.amlwchhistory.co.uk/data/placenames.htm
Wikipedia:	http://en.wikipedia.org/wiki/Welsh_placenames